A CANAD

BEST TAX HAVEN:

THE US

Take your money and DRIVE!

Robert Keats, CFP®, RFP, MSFP

Self-Counsel Press
(a division of)
International Self-Counsel Press Ltd.
USA   Canada

Self-Counsel Press acknowledges the financial support of the Government of Canada through the Canada Book Fund (CBF) for our publishing activities.

Printed in Canada.

First edition: 2012
Second edition: 2015

Library and Archives Canada Cataloguing in Publication

Keats, Robert
    A Canadian's best tax haven : the US : take your money and drive! / Robert Keats. — Second edition.

(Cross-border series)
Issued in print and electronic formats.
ISBN 978-1-77040-242-3 (pbk.).—ISBN 978-1-77040-858-6 (epub).—ISBN 978-1-77040-859-3 (kindle)

1. Tax havens. 2. Investments, Canadian—United States. 3. Tax planning—Canada. 4. Income tax—Canada. I. Title. II. Series: Cross-border series

K4464.5.K43 2015   336.2'06   C2015-900165-X
                                                 C2015-900166-8

Self-Counsel Press
(a division of)
International Self-Counsel Press Ltd.

Bellingham, WA	North Vancouver, BC
USA	Canada

Contents

3 The Hidden Cost of Traditional Tax Havens

4 Medical Considerations

7 The US Is an Incredible Tax Haven for Small-Business Owners

8 The Greatest Opportunities: Retirement Savings Plans

Samples and Illustrations

Notice to Readers

Laws are constantly changing. Every effort is made to keep this publication as current as possible. However, the author, the publisher, and the vendor of this book make no representations or warranties regarding the outcome or the use to which the information in this book is put and are not assuming any liability for any claims, losses, or damages arising out of the use of this book. The reader should not rely on the author or the publisher of this book for any professional advice. Please be sure that you have the most recent edition.

Prices, commissions, fees, and other costs mentioned in the text or shown in samples in this book may not reflect real costs where you live. Inflation and other factors, including geography, can cause the costs you might encounter to be much higher or even much lower than those we show. The dollar amounts shown are simply intended as representative examples.

Dedication

This book is dedicated to God and my family — wife: Barbara; children: Carl, Daniel, Sarah, and Rebekah; grandchildren: Daniel, Colton, and Addison. They all give my life meaning.

I would like to thank and express sincere appreciation for all of our cross-border clients and employees at KeatsConnelly for the support that has made the publication of this book possible.

Introduction

After writing ten editions of *The Border Guide: A Guide to Living, Working, and Investing across the Border*, a Canadian bestseller, and with about 1,000 Canadian baby boomers retiring each day, I felt the time was right for a simpler, more direct decision-making tool to assist Canadians in making the right choice when moving to a warmer climate in search of lower taxes.

This book will help you determine if the lifestyle choice of moving to a tropical climate with year-round golfing and sandy beaches is not only possible but whether it could also save you money, in the form of a lower cost of living and lower income taxes. This reduction in living expenses and taxes can allow you the ability to enjoy a lifestyle that most people have never dreamed possible.

The inspiration for this book came to me a few years ago when I was asked to speak to a group of Canadians in Dublin, Ireland. These Canadians were looking for the golden ticket — a tax haven which would allow them to more efficiently use their lifetime of savings to maintain that desired tropical lifestyle, without having to pay nearly half of their income to the government in the form of income taxes. At this conference, there were multiple lectures and seminars from major financial institutions from many of the major tax havens of the world, pontificating the benefits of moving to their jurisdictions.

Most of the attendees of this conference had read the book *Take Your Money and Run!* by Alex Doulis. He did an excellent job writing his book, and it was an interesting read that allowed readers to dream of living on a yacht or some tropical island free from any government-tax authority. He made it sound very romantic and exciting, but the bottom line is that it is totally impractical for most Canadians and would not likely result in any net cost of living and income tax reductions.

Who would want to live on a yacht bobbing up and down from port to port with nowhere to ever call home, all the while looking over his or her shoulder to make sure the tax man is not bearing down on him or her? It may be fine for a few people or for a little while; however, yachting is very difficult and expensive, not to mention confining, sometimes nauseating, and potentially dangerous. Similarly, trying to find that ideal tax haven island in the middle of nowhere is not very practical for most people for the multiple reasons I will outline in this book.

My 35 years of experience advising Canadians in international tax and financial planning matters told me that the desired tropical lifestyle and reduction in living expenses is available to most Canadians, literally right beneath their noses in the form of the United States of America. I'm also of the firm belief that you should "Give to Caesar what is Caesar's" (Mark 12:17) and that thumbing your nose at the Canada Revenue Agency (CRA), although sometimes tempting, does no one any good. Keeping the CRA on your side by following its negotiated treaty rules actually gives you greater freedom in your lifestyle choice and greater protection from an adversarial relationship that could cause you a lot of aggravation.

As you will see in this book, I am quite fed up and disheartened with a small contingent of Canadian advisors who have very little knowledge about US tax and financial planning rules but preach to clients as if they were experts. They clearly do not understand how the US can be used to assist Canadians in achieving their desired cross-border lifestyle and reducing taxes. In my opinion, these advisors take advantage of a trusted relationship with their clients. They continually perpetuate myths and provide the wrong advice about the US due to ignorance, personal bias, or just plain laziness to take time to get educated properly.

I make no apologies to those in the Canadian advisory industry who ignore the US when advising Canadians to take their money and go to the proverbial tax haven island in the middle of nowhere in an attempt to kiss the CRA goodbye. However, if they are sincerely interested in doing what is in the best interest of their clients, I encourage these advisors to read this book. By reading this book, they may change their perspectives and help clients make the right choice as to which option is more appropriate for them: the US, or the traditional tax haven island.

This book will show Canadians a practical path to that desired tropical lifestyle in a low-tax jurisdiction with full, protected access to Canada to invest, own a business, and visit family and friends without having to live on a rocky boat or an island in the middle of nowhere.

As with my authorship of *The Border Guide*, in order to prevent this book from becoming a dry technical manual that is factually accurate but functionally useless, I have presented my ideas in a non-technical fashion. Certain concepts have occasionally been simplified in the service of readability. Sound professional advice is unquestionably recommended for the application of any of the ideas, suggestions, or techniques detailed in *A Canadian's Best Tax Haven: The US*.

1

What Is a Tax Haven?

The words "tax haven" are indeed mysterious and sometimes misleading, and have oftentimes been used and abused to depict mystical and elusive dreams. What does it mean to go to a tax haven? Is it some sort of fortress, a beautiful island, or, perhaps, a nursing home?

There are many definitions for tax haven. There is a strict technical definition and then there is a simpler and easier to understand layperson's definition. I will describe both in this chapter, so you have a better insight into the world of tax havens. I will describe how you can cut through the mystery and get to the bottom line to see how you can benefit from the legal use of a tax haven, in particular the best tax haven for Canadians: the United States.

For Canadians, deciding to use a tax haven can be as simple as taking their money, packing their bags, and voting with their feet to depart Canada. In other words, Canadian citizens have no obligation to physically live in Canada to maintain their Canadian citizenship. When they leave Canada, they are no longer formal Canadian residents, and they are no longer subject to Canadian income taxes on their worldwide income. However, making that leap from Canadian residency to that of the tax haven can be a critical lifestyle choice, which warrants a great deal of research and planning before making that final move.

1. The Traditional Tax Haven

The traditional tax haven is defined as a country with the following characteristics:

- No or very minimal income tax.

- Bank secrecy to the extent the laws of the country will not allow the exchange of tax information or banking information with foreign authorities.

- Generally no tax treaty with any other country.

- Relative ease for a foreign person to establish residency with few immigration hurdles.

- No requirement for the resident to spend a minimum amount of time in that country, and the resident does not have to become a citizen.

- A stable government and political system backed by a significant police force and/or military.

2. The Real Tax Haven Definition

The following is the layperson's definition and the definition of the ideal tax haven I will use throughout this book:

An ideal tax haven is any country to which Canadians can easily move to achieve a preferred lifestyle whether it is better climate, lower taxes, or combination of both. This country will provide a lower overall individual cost of living by taking into consideration all factors such as food, accommodation, travel and including income tax, which will be less or substantially less than their current Canadian lifestyle costs. This country will still allow them to have the benefit of all of their Canadian family and social relationships while living in their preferred residence.

3. Where Are the Traditional Tax Havens?

Most of the so-called traditional tax havens used by Canadians are current or former British colonies and associated states located in the Caribbean. Approximately 15 percent of the countries in the world are considered traditional tax havens.

The following is a list of some of the more popular tax havens that fit the offshore traditional tax haven definition noted in section 1. and generally advertise themselves as tax havens:

- Bahamas.

- Bermuda.

- British Virgin Islands.

- Cayman Islands.

- Channel Islands.

- Cook Islands.

- Costa Rica.

- Cyprus.

- Isle of Man.

- Liechtenstein.

- Monaco.

- Panama.

- Seychelles.

- Switzerland.

- Turks and Caicos Islands.

Most of these traditional tax havens charge some level of income tax as well as other equivalent taxes or fees to those using the country as a resident or parking spot for assets (see section 4.). The International Monetary Fund (IMF) calculates that the combined cross-border assets of all these tax havens or Offshore Financial Centers (OSCs) — the new name for tax havens — constitute about 50 percent of the world's total cross-border assets or about $6 trillion.

Consequently, the impact these traditional tax havens have on the world economy is significant; particularly, taking into consideration the billions of dollars of annual income taxes individuals and corporations save using these OSCs that don't go into the coffers of their home countries and, thus, are available for capital investment around the world.

Each one of these tax havens has many different rules, taxes, fees, geographical limitations, and political stability issues. It makes it very difficult for most Canadians to use a traditional tax haven to their benefit because of the expenses, negative lifestyle choices, and geographical distance from Canada. You will read more about this in Chapters 2, 3, and 4.

4. The Taxes of Tax Havens

It could be considered an oxymoron for tax havens to have taxes but every country needs to pay its bills, so it is important to understand where tax havens take their money from individuals and corporations doing business in or through their country. I will give a few examples here for the more popular tax havens. This will give you a better feel for the type of taxes you would face from a traditional tax haven.

In addition to these various taxes and fees levied by a tax haven country, residents earning investment or business income outside the tax haven will face other non-resident withholding taxes on certain sources of income from other countries around the world; this kind of withholding is discussed further in Chapters 5 and 6.

The following sections include some typical examples of how traditional tax havens take in taxes from individuals living in their jurisdiction. It could be appropriate to go through all the other tax havens listed in section **3.** and give what would be a very similar series of direct and indirect taxes that those governments take from their residents and visitors. However, sections **4.1** and **4.2** give a very good idea of what you can expect from a traditional tax haven island.

Traditional tax havens vary in applicable rates and what they call their taxes to better conceal them from individual examination but they all have noteworthy taxes. These significant taxes can be a major cost factor that should be included in the decision of any Canadian looking to go to a traditional tax haven. In Chapter 3, I endeavor to give a typical estimation of the annual cost of living in traditional tax havens.

4.1 Bahamas

The government in the Bahamas taxes the following items:

- Property: Property tax is generally 1 percent of the assessed value of owner-occupied property annually and 1.5 percent of commercial property.

- Customs duties: Range from 0 to 210 percent and is collected on all imports. The average rate is 30 to 35 percent.

- Stamp duty: This is a flat-dollar or percentage tax on transactions such as land or personal property transfers, posting bonds, affidavits, and powers of attorney.

- Corporate taxes: Although corporations are not subject to a direct income tax, they are taxed on just about everything they do such as business licensing fees, import taxes, and inventory taxes.

- Foreign exchange control: Although not technically a tax, the foreign exchange control can be costly to those who are subject to it. Other than specific, capped amounts that may be handled by authorized banks, any transaction subject to the foreign exchange rules (e.g., loans, dividends, capital repatriation) must be approved by the central bank.

July 1, 2014 the Bahamas introduced a 15 percent value added tax, VAT, to allow it to reduce its import and excise duties to accommodate its submission into the World Trade Organization. The 15 percent VAT will be applied to all goods and services with the basic exemptions for things like food and health care. Although some of the customs duties noted in the second pull it point above may be decreased the overall net effect of the new VAT will mean higher total taxes.

4.2 Cayman Islands

The Cayman Islands taxes the following items:

- Imports: These duties range from 5 to 42 percent on virtually everything that comes to the islands. For example, luxury automobiles get the full 42 percent import duty.

- Tourist accommodation: This tax is around 10 percent.

- Financial institutions: Licensing fees range from $3,000 to $500,000 per year and tax on employees ranges from $500 to $20,000 per year per employee.

- Stamp duty: This duty on real estate purchases ranges from 7.5 to 9 percent of the value of the property. Mortgaging the property receives a 1.5 percent of the mortgage stamp duty. For rental property, it is 5 percent of the value of the property.

5. Mexico Is Generally Not Considered a Traditional Tax Haven

In the past several years Mexico has lost a great deal of its appeal because of thousands of murders annually due to the extensive gang wars and drug cartel activities that the Mexican government seems to slowly be getting under control. Although the media tends to blow things out of proportion as to what is actually happening, in many of the more desirable areas of Mexico, there is strong evidence that Canadians and other foreigners are not exempt from suffering the consequences of this gang warfare, including accidental death when caught in the cross-fire in cartel gun battles or kidnappings for ransom.

One of the main criteria to look for in a tax haven is that it has a well-established, stable government with a sufficient police force and/or army to keep the peace. The US has lower income taxes than both Canada and Mexico, a very good tax treaty with Canada, and a more stable system of government and police/armed forces than Mexico. In addition, the US, in many places, has a low cost of living equivalent to Mexico, so consequently most Canadians would agree the US Sun Belt and its tropical locations make the US a more suitable tax haven for Canadians.

Mexico has never been considered a traditional tax haven in the technical sense, which is why it was not in the list of world tax havens in section **3**. However, Mexico, with its lower cost of living and tax rates, does, to a certain extent, meet the layperson's definition of a tax haven. It does have a great deal of long sandy beaches, golf courses, palm trees, and seemingly endless days of summer. The great advantage of Mexico is in the cost of living where labor is plentiful and inexpensive, so a Canadian with an average income can live in substantial luxury.

Mexico has a Value Added Tax (VAT) of 16 percent on most goods and services in the country. As for income taxes, Mexico falls somewhere in between the US and Canada. Mexico's income taxes are not as high as Canada and not as low as the US on most types of income. Note that Mexican residents and nationals are taxed on their worldwide income.

Over many years of interviewing Canadians living in Mexico, I learned that the main tax savings come from the situation in which these people don't file the required Mexican tax returns and, therefore, unlawfully avoid Mexican income taxes. Even though the Mexican government is not all that sophisticated in catching people who are not filing the proper returns on their worldwide income, I believe those Canadians not in full compliance with Mexican tax laws are taking a substantial risk; they may be thrown in jail or have their assets seized if the Mexican government catches up to them.

As an advisor, I would never recommend you jeopardize your lifestyle and assets by going into a foreign jurisdiction and failing to comply with the tax regulations of that country with the hopes of never being caught. One day in a Mexican jail could easily be worse than 1,000 rainy days elsewhere. Flouting the law regardless of the chances of being caught is not a good tax haven strategy.

Note that Mexico has a tax treaty with Canada. If you follow Mexican tax rules, as you most definitely should, you will get some tax relief if you do decide to immigrate to Mexico and call it home.

6. The US Is a Good Tax Haven for Canadians

The US meets virtually all of the requirements of a good tax legal haven for Canadians but it is rarely mentioned when discussing worldwide tax havens.

As I mentioned in the introduction, I did a speech at a conference in Dublin, Ireland, several years ago. Many of the retired Canadians in attendance wanted to know if it was practical for them to go offshore to one of the traditional tax havens. They had savings and pensions they hoped would last them for a lifetime, particularly if they were prudent and made the right choice of jurisdiction to live in.

They were seeking the opportunity to get away from the Canadian combined income taxes, sales taxes, goods and services taxes (GST), harmonized sales taxes (HST, property taxes and land transfer taxes). All of these Canadian taxes when totaled were generally more than 50 percent of their income, which they had been forced to deal with their entire careers. These Canadians were seeking an answer to the question of whether there was relief available for them in retirement by moving to a tax haven, now that they had shed their businesses or jobs in Canada.

At the conference, the speakers mainly represented financial institutions from all the major tax havens and they spoke about the many possible tax benefits of their particular countries. The US as a tax haven never came up in any of the presentations to the Canadian group until I had my turn to speak. Initially, many thought I was crazy in my presentation even to mention the "United States" and "tax haven" in the same sentence!

The US is the most overlooked tax haven opportunity under the layperson's definition of this phrase as described in section 2, and the chapters to follow will provide convincing evidence of this.

6.1 Do not fear the Internal Revenue Service (IRS)

The Internal Revenue Service (IRS) is one of the main reasons most Canadians and many of their Canadian advisors never consider the US as a tax haven in which they can get substantial tax benefits. I wish I had a dollar for every time I heard a Canadian advisor tell his or her clients, "You don't want to move to the US because you'll have to deal with the IRS."

Over the years, the IRS has done one of the best negative marketing campaigns ever to get taxpayers to comply with its many complicated rules. It has developed an incredible brand that I would classify as "fearful respect." As an example, the Union Bank of Switzerland (UBS) had a recent scandal where the bank was discovered to be encouraging Americans to fraudulently hide money in their UBS Swiss bank accounts. The IRS had a very simple but effective negative campaign to get taxpayers to comply with its rules. The IRS put a couple of derelict taxpayers in jail and/or heavily fined them levied hundreds of millions of dollars in fines against the bank and then made sure the story was printed in every newspaper and discussed on every TV news station in the US, in Canada, and around the world!

The IRS was also successful in severely penalizing the UBS bank and forcing it to provide lists of all US citizens or residents with deposits in the UBS. Much to the mortification of the long-time Swiss government's highly coveted bank secrecy laws, this opened the doors for the IRS to force other banks in Switzerland and around the world to also provide lists of US citizens with deposits at their respective banks. The IRS was emboldened by the success with UBS and has attacked other Swiss banks in a similar manner, causing what has become a bit of a war between the IRS and Swiss banks, with many Swiss banks now refusing to allow any US citizens to open accounts at their banks.

The IRS scared US citizens and residents in a similar situation to the UBS scandal, who either deliberately or through ignorance failed to report to the IRS on deposits and investment accounts in foreign countries. The IRS then developed several amnesty programs for people to voluntarily come forward and disclose their foreign holdings, specifically called the Offshore Voluntary Disclosure Initiative (OVDI). Consequently, to avoid being thrown in jail, many US taxpayers subscribed to the amnesty program and had the penalties limited to about 20 percent of their offshore, previously non-reported assets rather than risk the IRS tracking them down.

These types of IRS campaigns are very effective in collecting funds by coercing taxpayers all over the US and the world to better comply with its rules voluntarily. In the two OVDI programs the IRS put out in 2009 and 2011, they collected close to $3 billion from thousands of US citizens, many of whom were also dual-citizen Canadians who, innocently, did not know of these foreign-reporting rules. A high-ranking IRS official bragged that this was the lowest cost and most successful tax collection program the IRS had ever conducted. . The latest voluntary disclosure program introduced in 2014 has allowed many filers living outside of the US, paying taxes in another country, who didn't understand the rules to get in compliance with reporting without any major penalties or fees.When you think about this, it is a brilliant branding campaign by the IRS; it costs virtually nothing but gets phenomenal attention and results. A corporation would spend many millions of dollars to get its branding up to the same level that the IRS can do virtually for free!

Canadians and their advisors take heed to the branding, and recognize the IRS as a force to be reckoned with, and avoid its ire where possible. This is exactly what the IRS wants: people to follow the rules and pay the taxes they are legally obligated to pay.

However, truth be known, for those who follow the rules and use them to their advantage, the IRS is as easy as or in many areas easier to deal with than the CRA. Taxpayers in the US have many more basic rights than taxpayers in Canada. For example, the IRS burden of proof standards prevent the IRS from attacking the taxpayer without solid proof that the person is in violation of statutes. These kinds of rules are in place to prevent the government from harassing taxpayers without sufficient evidence of any wrongdoing.

The IRS has a dispute resolution process that works very well to resolve complex or difficult tax assessments which cannot get resolved through the standard channel of calls, letters, and emails. This dispute resolution process is far superior, from the taxpayer's perspective, to the ombudsman program of the CRA. The IRS dispute resolution option allows the US taxpayer to bypass all the normal channels after a certain period of time of non-correction to get the problem resolved in a matter of weeks. Under CRA rules, whether or not you are right or wrong, some problems seem to go unresolved with a great deal of time and expense wasted unnecessarily by both the taxpayer and CRA.

I do not know whether it is just my imagination or paranoia but there seems to be a definite change in CRA over the past several years with its appeals officers and auditors. From my observation, the employees have become very aggressive and less willing to negotiate with Canadian taxpayers over disputes. This change of attitude by the CRA dramatically increases the taxpayers' legal and other costs to fight for their rights. Often the only practical solution is to do what the CRA is demanding even though the CRA may be wrong. In contrast, in the US, if the IRS is wrong or overly aggressive and impinges on common sense and logic in proceedings against taxpayer, including violation of the taxpayer rights the taxpayer has the full right to recover all of their legal expenses from the IRS all based on the decision of an independent judge.

There are more taxpayer rights in the US; however, the IRS, similar to the CRA, is no picnic to deal with under the best of circumstances. My main point is, for those who generally follow the rules and do not push filing options past prudent limitations, chances of a timely and favorable resolution of tax problems are better in the US when dealing with the IRS, than they are in Canada when dealing with CRA.

Taxpayers, along with their Canadian advisors, should not fear the IRS any more or less than the CRA unless they are intentionally breaking tax rules or are planning to do so. In Chapter 9, I return to this topic as many Canadian advisors create and perpetuate the myth of avoiding the US because of the IRS in order to discourage Canadians from looking at the US as their tax haven.

6.2 The current US economic environment

There has been an overabundance of media hype recently concerning the economic condition of the US with many doomsday scenarios. There is no doubt that some of the concerns and fears expressed are real. What are the long-term effects going to be and should this deter any Canadians from using the US as their desired tropical lifestyle and tax haven?

There are numerous opinions, scenarios, and theories as to what will be the consequences of the US not getting a grip on its ballooning debt and continued government spending. Most logical observers would agree that the US does have to do something relatively soon to deal with these concerns. How the US deals with these concerns is probably where the focus of people's attention should be. Optimism is hard to find in this negative news media barrage; however, I believe the US will both survive and thrive through this crisis for the following reasons:

- The US remains the largest free economy in the world.

- At the very hint of any crisis anywhere in the world, investors continually rush to the US dollar and US treasuries as the safest place to hold their funds.

- Similar to Canada in the 1990s, the governments of Greece, Italy, and Spain in 2011 came to the realization they must take decisive and painful actions to reduce their debt burden down to manageable levels. I'm sure the US government will come to that point soon if they haven't already.

- The US has the largest gold reserve of any country in the world and the value of gold has increased over the past decade.

- The US federal government is considered the biggest landlord in the world, controlling billions of dollars of commercial land and properties.

- The US continues to lead the world in innovation creating some of the largest and most successful corporations such as Apple, Google, Facebook, Coca-Cola, McDonald's, Walmart, IBM, and Boeing.

- The US continues to be the destination of choice for immigrants from around the world, most of whom are very well educated.

- The US has been rated the most charitable country in the world (Charity Aid Foundation's World Giving Index: December, 2013).

- The latest in oil and gas drilling technology and the new discoveries in the Dakotas have made the US the largest energy producer in the world once more, which means that the US, in a very short time, will no longer need to import oil from the Middle East or other areas of the world other than Canada. This low cost energy source has enabled high consumption of energy type manufacturing to start moving back to the US creating more jobs and reducing the US unemployment rate close to 2007 levels.

- For Canadians moving to the US, the Canada-US Tax Treaty allows them to keep assets in Canada or Canadian securities purchased through US financial institutions without any adverse Canadian income tax consequences.

In short, Canadians looking to the US as their tax haven need not be concerned any more or less than they are with the goings-on with the Canadian government. As described in later chapters, most of the benefits of using the US as a tax haven stem from the fact that the Canada-US Tax Treaty has fixed rates that almost never change regardless of what the Canadian or US government decide to do.

7. Canada Is a Tax Haven

Believe it or not, Canada is considered a tax haven by some individuals from around the world. An article in Maclean's (July 2011) titled "The Great White Tax Haven" opened the eyes of Canadians to the possibility that some foreigners consider Canada a legitimate tax haven.

When an individual moves across international borders from one country's tax jurisdiction to another, creative but legitimate planning can generate many tax-reduction opportunities that would not be available had the person remained in his or her home country without emigration to another. This peculiar paradox prevents Canadians from using Canada as a tax haven and Americans from using the US as a tax haven; Canadians cannot take advantage of the CRA's tax haven rules by remaining in Canada and, similarly, US citizens cannot take advantage of the US tax haven opportunities Canadians have in moving to the US.

8. An End to the Traditional Tax Haven?

The past decade has seen a worldwide assault on traditional tax havens in an attempt to expose those who are fraudulently hiding money from their legitimate tax regimes in their home country. The main thrust of this attack has been from the G20 (the group of the top 20 free-world countries in terms of economic impact) and the Organisation for Economic Co-operation and Development (OECD). The central focus of the attacks have been on forcing tax havens into information exchange with the pretense of preventing tax havens from being used illegally by citizens of various countries around the world. By allowing people to hide money, the tax havens gain an unfair economic advantage over the industrialized countries that generate the wealth that their respective citizens sometimes feel they must hide secretly in the tax havens.

For example, the G20 has developed a tax-haven blacklist to force tax havens into cooperating with an internationally agreed-upon tax standard. Tax havens that fail to cooperate with these information-sharing standards remain on the tax-haven blacklist and face significant sanctions from the G20.

Because of this pressure from the G20, nearly every major overseas financial center has agreed to the OECD standards since 2008. With the collapse of Lehman Brothers, and with financial markets crashing around the world, governments were forced to bail out stricken financial institutions. With ballooning debts, the governments stepped up the pressure against offshore financial centers and tax evasion. Effectively, there are fewer and fewer countries of consequence in the world for tax evaders to hide. The effect on traditional tax havens is yet to be determined, as all this forced cooperation has happened so quickly and so recently the full effects are difficult to predict.

Individual countries have also used their own legislative processes and economic leveraging to force tax havens to exchange banking information pertaining to its citizens. New US income tax rules, called the Foreign Account Tax Compliance Act (FATCA), require financial institutions around the world to disclose information about US citizens who hold financial accounts at their respective institutions, or the institution will risk withholding taxes of 30 percent on all payments on all outbound income from their US investments held by the particular financial institution refusing to comply. The FATCA requirements have been nearly fully implemented in 2014 and with these rules, many more dual-citizen Canadian residents or US citizens living abroad in other countries will be identified to the US authorities and could face harsh penalties on money they may no longer have. Following right behind the US lead the UK, France, Canada and Germany have also recently introduced new legislation to force their respective citizens and the financial institutions that they deal with worldwide into compliance with the tax rules.

The positive results from all of these worldwide pressures on tax havens is that legitimate cross-border enterprises and individual cross-border migration will happen as it should, using fully legitimate domestic and tax-treaty rules. This is a huge boost for Canadians who are not trying to evade taxes but only trying to legally avoid them through voting with their feet. Even though there are many of these above-noted new rules to follow, the rules in themselves, when followed closely, give a greater sense of security.

Even though I'm not a big fan of more rules, I do like to use rules to assist clients in providing clarity and increased certainty that legitimate cross-border planning and tax-reduction plans can succeed. Fortunately, many of these new rules accomplish that and provide better planning opportunities.

Why Traditional Tax Havens Don't Work

If I have learned anything from my many years of providing financial advice to families of all types, sizes, and levels of wealth, it is that lifestyle and family needs trump tax planning nearly every single time. Once people get to a certain level of wealth (which is subjective and different for every individual), the amount of taxes they pay and their cost of living goes down several notches in priority in favor of family decision-making. The preferred lifestyle appropriately rises to become the primary criteria in deciding where they are going to live, with tax reduction and cost-of-living reduction in the background. I firmly believe this pecking order of priorities is not only the correct one, but also the one that leads to the happiest and most well-balanced individuals and families.

It makes very little sense for a family to work hard over their lifetime to generate the level of wealth that they desire and then not be able to live the lifestyle they choose. They need to enjoy the wealth rather than be caught up in a complicated tax-haven scheme that dictates where, how, and when they can enjoy their wealth. It is for this reason that traditional tax havens often fail to help people fulfill their lifestyle dreams.

1. A Tale of Two Business Partners

An exceptionally good example of why the traditional tax haven on the proverbial island in the middle of nowhere just doesn't work for most families is that of two long-time business partners who, in 2005, sold their very successful business in Canada[1]. This particular example was almost like someone set it up on purpose for a research study to see what two families with roughly the same set of circumstances and net worth did over time with their wealth, using two very different paths and two very different sets of advisors.

These two partners equally owned their business in Canada and each received in excess of $30 million before tax from the sale of the business. They were both married and the first partner, John, and his wife, Mary, came to my firm, KeatsConnelly, because they wanted to live in Arizona now that they were no longer tied to the business. Fortunately, they came to us prior to the closing of the sale of the business so that we could implement their plan and include all available options.

The second partner, Mike, and his wife, Sally, hired one of the big-four accounting firms in Canada who advised them to go offshore to the traditional tax haven island of Grand Cayman.

Fast forward to 2014 and we could see the net result of which couple saved the most taxes because of their very different advice and lifestyle choices, and which couple is most content with their lifestyle choice now.

Mike and Sally were visiting John and Mary recently at their home in Arizona and Mike, seeing his partner's comfortable lifestyle, started asking questions about how he could do the same. John gave Mike my phone number. When Mike talked with me, he stated he was tired of living in the Cayman Islands. He found the lifestyle boring and the entire idea of living on a distant island was getting very old. This island, although very beautiful, had lost its romantic appeal yielding to the impracticality of living on an island from both a lifestyle and tax perspective. Mike was a bit uncomfortable with the amount of time he and Sally were spending in both Canada and the United States visiting friends and relatives. He was worried that Canada Revenue Agency (CRA) and the Internal Revenue Service (IRS) might come after him, and he felt he was always looking over his shoulder waiting for the other shoe to drop. Mike was looking for advice on how he could get set up like his former partner, John, in Arizona and he was already looking at buying a house in a development near John.

---

1 In this example, and all of the other real examples and situations used in this book, I have changed names, places, details, and numbers to protect the confidentiality of the actual people involved.

By talking with Mike and his financial advisors I determined several remarkable facts. The first fact was that Mike, even though he went to the traditional island tax haven, paid substantially more income tax on his half of the sale of the business upon his exit from Canada, versus John who used the US as his tax haven. The primary reason Mike paid more tax was that the Cayman Islands has no tax treaty with Canada.

Mike's financial advisors ignored the US for Mike's tax-reduction options. John, being a resident of the US, was able to take advantage of the lower Canada-US Tax Treaty rates to withdraw his funds from Canada. Although John did pay taxes on the sale of his share of the business to the CRA, he was able to recover them entirely from the IRS through the IRS Foreign Tax Credit rules. The net result from a tax perspective was that Mike paid approximately $5 million more in income taxes than John on exactly the same transaction. How ironic is it that Mike's advisors sent him to a traditional tax haven yet he paid an incredible amount more in income taxes than his former partner did by going to the US.

Some of the other facts revealed by Mike were that he and Sally were spending a substantial amount of time in Canada and the US. Because of regularly visiting family and spending time in Canada, they had inadvertently established several residential ties with Canada, which made them vulnerable to the CRA. If the CRA discovered these residential ties and determined Mike and Sally were Canadian residents, they would be subject to the full Canadian rates of income tax on their worldwide income. There would be a great deal of potential income tax and penalties due if they lost the CRA challenge to their residency. Even if they were able to keep CRA at bay after a potential challenge to residency, the entire defending process would be extremely stressful and very costly since Canada has no treaty with the Cayman Islands.

Mike and Sally were also making several annual trips from the Cayman Islands to Florida for medical treatment and to escape the boredom of island living. (The largest Cayman Island, Grand Cayman, is less than 20 miles long and a mile or two wide in most places, with a total population of about 50,000.) This time spent by Mike and Sally in the US was very limited and they had to count the days they spent there, to ensure they were not going to be considered taxable residents by the IRS under the IRS substantial presence rules.

Although the Cayman Islands have no personal income tax, Mike found that when he invested in his favorite US and Canadian stocks, the withholding tax he faced on the dividends was higher than the actual tax he would pay if he was living in the US - 30 percent nonresident withholding tax versus 23.8 percent maximum regular tax. In the US, John was able to receive interest, tax free, in similar amounts to Mike in the Caymans. (Chapter 6 discusses the myth that Canadians pay less tax in traditional tax havens than they would if they lived in the US.)

Mike also was tired of all the import taxes and other taxes he constantly had to pay, which cost him many thousands of dollars a year that John did not have to pay in the US. It really irked Mike that John could purchase the same Mercedes in Arizona for $50,000 less than he paid for his Mercedes in the Cayman Islands.

Mike and Sally also found that John and Mary were not forced to travel extensively just to go for entertainment; attend doctor's appointments; or to visit their children, parents, and grandchildren. John and Mary could hop on a nonstop flight from Phoenix to Calgary and be there in three hours, whereas for Mike and Sally to travel from the Cayman Islands to Calgary it was a full day of travel, full of frustration with connecting flights at several airports. If Mike and Sally's friends and family wanted to visit them, a large part of their vacation was taken up in travel time — long weekend trips were out of the question. John and Mary could travel to Canada as much as they wanted without fear of the CRA treating them as residents of Canada and, therefore, they were automatic nonresidents of Canada which made them subject to tax only in the US. (The Canada-US Tax Treaty protection for individuals or couples like John and Mary, as US residents, is explained in Chapter 5.) As Cayman Island residents, Mike and Sally had no treaty protection whatsoever and they were very vulnerable to CRA or the IRS attempting to tax them as residents of each respective country.

Fortunately, for Mike and Sally, they can still follow John and Mary to Arizona to enjoy a similar relaxed and lower cost lifestyle, with the year-round warm sunshine they desire. It is unfortunate though that Mike and Sally paid such a high price in both taxes and diminished lifestyle for nearly 10 years. They, in effect, gave up the best lifestyle they may have chosen to chase the elusive tax savings of the Cayman Islands and their tax savings were not as great as John and Mary's. Therefore, as long as Mike's financial advisors didn't scare him into avoiding the IRS rules rather than embracing them, by 2015 he and Sally would have been fully installed in Arizona enjoying the lifestyle they actually tried to achieve ten years previous by moving to the Cayman Islands.

2. The United States Is the Only Tax Haven to Which Canadians Can Drive

A very important factor in choosing a place to live, is to find one which allows you to improve upon your existing relationships to the extent desired and to live your preferred lifestyle.

For a great number of Canadians I find the most favorable lifestyle choice is generally maintaining the Canadian family homestead or home base (this homestead can be large, small, rented, owned, or an in-law suite at a relative's) near where the majority of the family is or was located. This allows for summertime fun in Canada and an equally or nicer home in a warm sunny tropical climate in which the family can spend their time during long, cold Canadian winters. The family can have access to a perpetual summer with as little or no snow to shovel as they desire.

Ultimately, there must be an ease of travel between the chosen abodes. This allows family members to drive easily to a destination or for them to have plenty of choices for nonstop airline flights so travel is relatively short, painless, and economical. As Mike and Sally found out the hard way, a tax haven which is an island in the middle of nowhere does not come close to fitting these requirements, and their preferred lifestyle couldn't be realized to the fullest.

It is a well-known fact that 90 percent of the Canadian population lives within 150 kilometers of the US border. This means that most Canadians are a one- to two-hour drive from their best potential tax haven. Those who choose not to drive have numerous other travel options that allow very easy access to almost any desired major US Sun Belt location. It is much less expensive to fly from just about anywhere in Canada to anywhere in the southern US than it is to fly within Canada from Victoria to Toronto.

This ease of travel to and from the US should not be underestimated. One of the biggest complaints Canadians have going to one of the traditional tax haven islands is that in most cases their only options are to fly with sometimes more than one connecting flight on a puddle-jumper aircraft. These limited travel options are exacerbated when there's a medical emergency, particularly if the patient's not able to travel by air to the US or to Canada to get potentially lifesaving medical assistance.

An important criticism I have heard from Canadians who have gone to and from an offshore island is that they have left their adult children and grandchildren in Canada. These difficult travel hurdles become a real detriment to family get-togethers and important family events such as weddings, reunions, bar mitzvahs, births, and funerals. From just about anywhere in Western Canada it is a frustrating full day of travel to any Caribbean island or other traditional tax haven, even if everything goes well. How many times would parents with young children want to make this exhausting trip across three or four time zones? It is only marginally better when traveling from Toronto or Montreal to these islands.

The opposite is true when traveling from Calgary, Edmonton, or Vancouver to Phoenix, San Diego, Las Vegas, Los Angeles, or Palm Springs. Similarly, from Montreal and Toronto there are many daily nonstop flights to Phoenix, Los Angeles, Tampa, Palm Beach, Fort Lauderdale, Fort Myers, Orlando, or Miami. Even though there are numerous daily nonstop flights between these cities, if you wanted to drive, the drive can usually be easily accomplished in two or three days. If you do not want to drive, you can ship your car for a few hundred dollars back and forth each winter, none of this would be possible between any Canadian city and any traditional tax haven island.

For those who actually wish to live on a tropical island, and at the same time use the US as their tax haven, the US has many island options such as Hawaii, Puerto Rico, US Virgin Islands, and the Florida Keys.

2.1 Easy commute

I have one client, Jerry, who leaves his family in Arizona and commutes weekly to Alberta to work in his business for four days, then returns to Arizona for three days. Because of his frequent flying, he normally gets free first-class upgrades for his less than three-hour nonstop flights to Alberta and back. Jerry has a beautiful house with a swimming pool, on a large lot with many citrus trees and palm trees in a great Arizona neighborhood.

The cost of his Arizona home is less than half of what a similarly sized house in Alberta, with no pool and no palm or citrus trees cost him. Even though Jerry's home is in a relatively expensive neighborhood in the Phoenix area, Jerry's property taxes for a bigger house with more amenities are less than those of his Alberta home.

When Jerry sells his business, because of his ability to use the US as a tax haven, he will likely be able to save a great deal in income taxes. Therefore, not only does he get the lifestyle he desires, he benefits with a reduction in taxes better than he could get if he moved his family to one of the traditional tax haven islands.

2.2 Buying or building your dream home

Purchasing or building a dream home in the US Sun Belt is similar to purchasing or building a home in Canada. Building materials, construction techniques, and construction workers would all be much more familiar to you in the US than they would be in an island country. In fact, most wealthy Canadians at some point in their lives have purchased or constructed US real estate long before considering the US as a potential tax haven.

One pleasant surprise to Canadians using the US as their tax haven is that the purchase of a new residence in the US may actually be much less expensive than an equivalent property in Canada. The same cannot be said for most offshore jurisdictions.

If you are building your home in an offshore tax haven, materials need to be brought in by boat which makes the selection of building materials both limited and expensive. Similarly, new furniture and appliances may need to be shipped in, usually with a great deal of import tax, if you have a particular preference for a brand or style.

3. Disadvantages of Traditional Tax Havens

The following list discusses some of the disadvantages of traditional tax havens:

- Any personal relationships with family or friends are bound to suffer with the traditional tax-haven strategy, because of the geography of living on an island in the middle of nowhere, or bouncing around from port to port on a yacht attempting to keep ahead of the proverbial tax man.

- The assumption that there are no taxes in offshore jurisdictions is a myth.

- Canadian dividends and trust income originating in Canada face Canadian withholding taxes at 25 percent.

- There is a 30 percent withholding tax from the IRS for US-sourced dividends and similar income.

- Switzerland takes 35 percent withholding on trust income and dividends for residents of tax havens with no treaty protection.

- Canada's Old Age Security (OAS) is subject to the 100 percent claw-back tax rate and/or nonresident withholding tax of 25 percent that can reduce this pension to zero for both spouses. This one tax alone can produce a potential loss of more than $13,000 a year for a couple.

- Canada Pension Plan (CPP) and other pensions are subject to a 25 percent nonresident withholding tax.

- RRSP and RRIF income as a nonresident is also subject to the 25 percent nonresident withholding.

- Before departing Canada, you are subject to a departure or exit tax on the day you leave Canada on certain taxable Canadian assets that have unrealized capital gains and yet-to-be-taxed capital gains. Although these taxes can be deferred by giving the CRA suitable collateral, there is a great deal of paperwork and hassle to deal with these exit taxes effectively.

- Food and housing costs on islands are higher than in the US or Canada. Also, the selection and availability of foods and other consumer goods are much more limited. This cost-of-living increase reduces and often negates potential tax savings of traditional tax havens and the lack of choice noticeably reduces your lifestyle enjoyment.

- Simple things such as setting up bank accounts and credit cards become surprisingly complex when trying to do it through an offshore tax haven.

3.1 Get me off of this island!

Several years back, an Albertan man who had a net worth in the nine-digit range was looking for tax relief on his extremely high income. He approached the typical large Canadian accounting and law firms for help and they sent him to one of the offshore Caribbean tax-haven islands. He lasted only six months on the island before he was bored stiff from talking to the locals at the corner bar about fishing or other things that mattered little to him. He came charging back to Canada, saying, "I don't care what tax I have to pay; I'm not going to be imprisoned on an island!"

Had this individual's advisors spent time understanding the life-planning issues important to him, they would've found that a move to the US would likely have been more appropriate to balance his desired lifestyle while at the same time affording him most, or even all, the tax benefits of the island tax haven. One of the major problems I find when planning with typical accountants and lawyers, is that they get so involved in the numbers game they forget they are dealing with real people who have real lives and families!

3.2 Tax havens are treaty deficient

Since traditional tax havens have no tax treaty with Canada, there is consequently no treaty protection (see Chapter 5). Canadian taxpayers who exit Canada to live in a traditional tax haven must clearly sever all residential ties and leave nothing they own in Canada. They should not even visit Canada for the first two years, and then only on a very short-term basis to ensure the CRA does not try to deem them to be residents of Canada, obliterating all of their critical tax planning.

Without treaty protection, it is quite easy for the CRA to use the most minor of issues to deem an ex-Canadian resident still a taxpayer in Canada and attempt to tax him or her as if he or she never left Canada. Something as minor as leaving furniture in storage in Canada, holding a Canadian driver's license, or leaving a vehicle in Canada can send the CRA on a rampage to tax the expatriate as a full Canadian resident.

Moving to an offshore tax haven is a major and disruptive lifestyle change for most Canadians, and it often raises the question, "Why have we worked so hard all our lives to obtain financial independence and then not be able to choose the lifestyle we want?" However, when these Canadians choose the US as the tax haven they are entitled to follow the tiebreaker rules of the Canada-US Tax Treaty (more on this in Chapter 5). Canadian travel and personal ties with Canada are not nearly as much of a concern based on the great deal of protection taxpayers have from the treaty, if the CRA were to attack a Canadian's residency status in the US. Their lifestyles need to change very little, particularly if they already had a primary residence in the US where they have been going during the winter for many years already.

In summary, lifestyle and life-planning needs for individuals are important, and advisors who ignore these issues in favor of tax savings from some far-off island will inevitably result in very unhappy clients much like Mike and Sally (described in section 1. of this chapter).

3.3 Culture shock

The culture shock of going to a faraway tax-haven island or country can be a major adjustment for most people and should not be underestimated. If you want somewhere to call home for possibly the rest of your life, you must have a culture fit for the lifestyle you desire. Depending on where you come from in Canada, English or French is not always the local language of traditional tax havens, which can be a disadvantage for some people in a new country.

The main advantage the US has over a number of the tax havens is that English is the primary language. For Canadians choosing the US as a tax haven, other than dropping a few "ehs" and adding a few more "you alls," there is no adjustment period or language difficulties when understanding and dealing with the local population.

3.4 Problems receiving proper medical treatment

Medical facilities, procedures, and professional practitioners are very similar between Canada and the US. Many Canadian and American doctors and nurses are trained at the same facilities. Consequently, there is little adjustment to make when receiving or understanding US medical treatments and options.

My experience with persons who have gone offshore is that they have had considerable difficulty getting proper medical treatment and access to familiar facilities and procedures. In most cases, these people return to Canada or go to the US for treatment, so they risk jeopardizing their tax-haven status.

3.5 Owning a vehicle in a foreign country

It goes without saying that Americans drive on the same side of the road as Canadians in vehicles that are virtually identical. Consequently, Canadians can simply import their vehicles to the US when they take up residency there without any concern other than government paperwork. This would be a near impossibility if the taxpayers were going to an offshore tax haven; the vehicles they owned in Canada would have to be sold, often at a loss. The new vehicle they would need to obtain on the island may have the steering wheel on the opposite side of the vehicle, with different manufacturers and options, and may have to be purchased at an outrageous price. Note that vehicles have to be imported to an island so prices are much higher.

A purchase of a vehicle in the US, in the majority of cases, is less expensive than the identical vehicle in Canada. Note that in the US you won't have to pay GST or HST on your vehicle purchase; a 5 percent cost advantage at minimum.

There are far fewer lifestyle adjustments with far fewer unpleasant surprises for Canadians moving to the US Sun Belt than for Canadians choosing to go to a traditional tax-haven island. There are substantial savings in costs for Canadians purchasing homes and vehicles in the US versus the traditional tax haven; these cost savings can be significant and add to the hidden costs which I define as the "hidden taxes" for Canadians not using the US as their primary tax haven. (Chapter 3 identifies these hidden costs in more detail.)

The Hidden Cost of Traditional Tax Havens

When Canadians and their advisors discuss tax havens, the center of attention is often the tax reduction. This focus masks a major tax-haven cost as it relies on the assumption the cost of living and the cost of doing business is the same for the tax haven as it is in other countries such as the United States. This often leads to many unpleasant surprises that are added to the myriad hidden costs such as building or buying a home or buying an automobile, which was discussed in Chapter 2. However, the extra cost of housing and transportation pales in comparison to the cost of doing business when you move to an offshore tax haven island rather than the US.

This major cost or what I might more appropriately call the "real hidden tax of traditional tax havens" is the cost of managing your financial affairs while living offshore. Even though these costs are technically not a tax, they most certainly have the same effect as a tax in that they reduce the net available spending income provided by investment portfolios. These costs manifest themselves in numerous ways, such as the following:

- Investment management fees.
- Security trading costs.
- Legal costs.

- Accounting fees.
- Wealth management fees.
- Trustee fees.
- Security spreads or markups.
- Custodial fees.

Most of these costs are what traditional tax havens depend on to be financially viable. After all, these traditional tax havens customarily do not charge any personal income taxes, so they need to have a source of income to run their country.

1. Full Disclosure Inadequate in Tax Havens

I am a proponent of full disclosure; if you give consumers all of the facts as to what it's costing them to do something, they can make educated decisions and they can understand what they are paying for. Unfortunately, banks and brokerage firms in the US, in Canada, and in offshore financial centers, have many ways of taking money from the consumers' pockets without disclosing their methods to the public. Disclosure to the investment public is not perfect in the US; there are still several areas in need of improvement, particularly with brokerage firms.

Predominantly, in tax havens but also in both Canada and the US, brokerage firms are not required to act in the best interest of consumers. They are allowed to sell anything they deem suitable, charge fees, and take investment markups and spreads behind the scenes in numerous ways that often work against consumers and may not be disclosed to them completely. Canada has some new rules coming into effect in 2015 that will go a long way to close this disclosure gap.

Brokerage firm self-dealing and pushing shaky product sales was one of the major contributors to the 2008/2009 financial collapse. Brokerage firms were selling near-worthless mortgage-backed US securities to consumers, which the firms had rated AAA. The firms then took the opposite or ostensible short position in their own portfolios to profit when these so-called AAA securities started to collapse and become worthless. The brokerage firms, at least in the US, are still being heavily fined for their fraudulent disclosures, but not necessarily their customer sales suitability.

Investment management and administration costs, whether fully disclosed or not, are not unique to offshore tax havens. However, because of the less refined, scarce, or inadequate regulations and disclosure laws in the traditional tax haven, the consumer can be taken advantage of. I consistently see consumers using financial institutions in these off-shore tax havens oblivious to the costs associated with using them. There is generally nowhere for them to go to demand more disclosure or to complain about shortcomings. As many people have found in these tax havens, the communities are close knit and, very often, the people providing you the services are the same people or relatives of the ones that make the rules.

2. US Registered Investment Advisors Provide the Best Consumer Protection

Both in Canada and the US there are several websites where consumers can review public disclosure documents such as prospectuses of mutual funds and exchange traded funds, which detail all of the fees and expenses charged by the funds. In the US, the Securities and Exchange Commission (SEC) has a website where you can get complete backgrounds and full disclosure on how a firm or an individual Registered Investment Advisor (RIA) manages portfolios. These resources provide full disclosure on how RIAs charge their fees, what their educational background and experience is, potential conflicts of interest, and any prior regulatory breaches for each individual or corporation in the country that holds themselves out as investment advisors or financial planners managing money.

The RIAs in the US are required to act in a fiduciary capacity, which means they must put consumers' and clients' interests ahead of their own at all times. The same cannot be said for unregistered investment advisors in the US, Canada, and offshore brokerage firms; as noted in section 1., they can sell whatever they deem suitable without the fiduciary standard; in other words, they can act on their own or in their company's best interest rather than the consumers'.

For brokerage firms and brokers in the US there are good websites where you can get regulatory violation histories for the firms and their sales brokers. A Google search of US brokerage firms or RIA disclosures will bring up the government-sponsored websites to assist consumers in the US.

The disclosure requirements for security transactions in offshore tax havens are limited, particularly when compared with those in the US. This allows investment managers to take fees and self-deal without the necessary consumer protection regulations forcing them to disclose or act in a fiduciary capacity for the clients. These offshore tax haven facilitators can take advantage of the situation and charge much higher fees in a manner that they would never get away with in the US.

In the US, the regulations by the SEC force all independent financial advisors, RIAs, not only to charge reasonable fees but also to disclose all fees and conflicts of interest to their clients. To make sure the advisors are complying, they are subjected to surprise audits. Most offshore tax haven islands will have no, or very limited, regulatory oversight to assist with consumer protection.

3. Brokerage Firms Are Not Required to Act in the Consumer's Best Interest

Brokerage firms are not required to act in the consumer's best interest with full disclosure regardless of the millions of dollars in TV advertising they spend trying to convince you otherwise. That is the crux of a major regulatory debate in the US as to whether brokerage firms should be held to the higher standard that the Registered Investment Advisors (RIAs) already subscribe to under the Securities and Exchange Commission (SEC) regulations. Most financial services consumers do not understand that when it comes to protection, there is a substantial difference between brokerage firms and RIAs. Simply put, brokerage firms can legally act in their own self-interest whereas RIAs must act in the consumer's best interest.

The large big-name brokerage firms in the US are very profitable and have a great deal of money available to fight legislation. They use these funds to hire lobbyists to try to consolidate the power to prevent them from being held to the higher fiduciary standard that helps protect consumers. The long and short of it is, anyone who is looking for independent investment advice in the US should avoid large brokerage firms or at least understand how they are not legally required to act in the consumer's best interest. The best alternative is to talk to an RIA individual or firm that is regulated under the SEC. There are thousands of RIA firms in the US so they are relatively easy to find.

4. Tax Haven Advisor Background Information Is Scarce

When using traditional tax haven islands and offshore financial centers you will normally find it very difficult to get background information on the corporations or individuals you may be dealing with. Unlike the US, there are very few websites that are available in the regulatory environment of these offshore tax havens that give full disclosure on the products being sold and the people selling them or managing portfolios. For some reason, these offshore financial institutions expect people to trust them because they are a tax haven, yet consumers could be dealing with someone who has a security violation or fraud in his or her background.

5. Focusing on the Fees

The remainder of this chapter will focus on fees; primarily on the principal fees that almost every investor will deal with by becoming a resident of a traditional tax haven. This information can be proven by public data that is readily available if any prudent investor chooses to seek disclosure of these fees.

This section will also cover investment management and trading cost of an investment strategy, primarily in public markets as available from traditional tax-haven money managers, banks, and brokers. These are the costs of simply maintaining a large investment portfolio, which the majority of individuals or families going offshore would most likely have. Generally, this large portfolio of wealth was likely created by some major family liquidating event such as selling a successful business, using lifetime savings, or receiving an inheritance. Often this wealth is what triggers the Canadian advisor's recommendation for the client to consider going to an offshore tax haven. Consequently, this managed portfolio can be very significant in size and, therefore, costly to look after, given that it is probably the family nest egg meant to keep the family going for generations.

5.1 Management expense ratio (MER)

An actively managed offshore mutual fund portfolio of investments of virtually any combination and type of stocks and bonds typically averages management fees of 2.5 percent annually. These fees are generally called management expense ratios (MERs). These funds have trading costs and other administrative costs normally around 1 percent annually. When all administrative costs are included, the MER can total around 3.5 percent per year. These annual costs can easily exceed this already high threshold of 3.5 percent, depending on the type of actively managed funds. Several so-called specialty funds can reach in the 4 to 5 percent range.

Portfolios of managed bonds or bond funds are usually less costly than the actively managed stock funds. Offshore bond funds typically have MERs ranging from 1.5 to 2.5 percent per year.

Fees and commissions on these kinds of actively managed stock and bond funds are very similar to Canadian funds since most Canadians use a Canadian offshore bank of some sort in a tax-haven jurisdiction. These actively managed mutual funds are the sales product of choice by the brokerage firms associated with Canadian banks primarily because they pay the highest commissions. However, several other portfolio management setups are available in offshore tax havens.

5.2 Undisclosed security markups

Another popular choice for investment management in offshore financial institutions might be a bank or brokerage that offers its own portfolio of individual stocks and bonds. These offshore financial institutions may disclose to you that the management fee is only 1 to 1.5 percent per year. Most offshore investment consumers, when asked, would say that this 1 to 1.5 percent was the only cost they paid for their portfolio management without understanding there are several hidden costs not disclosed.

In this individual stock and bond portfolio strategy, hidden costs can range from 50 to 100 percent or more of the disclosed management fee. As mentioned at the beginning of this chapter, some of these nondisclosed or hidden fees can include:

- Brokerage commissions.
- Security spreads or markups.
- Trustee fees.
- Administrative fees.
- Custodian fees.

A typical example of these nondisclosed fees is the spread or markup investors pay for their individual bonds. The broker or manager purchases bonds on the open market, adds 1 to 5 percent onto the price of the bond over what he or she buys them for, and then sells them to the consumer at the marked up price; the broker or manager pockets the difference. This purchase would normally show up as one price on the client brokerage statement, showing only the marked up price as being the purchase price of the bond with no disclosure of how much markup the brokerage firm took on the transaction. Unless the consumer is very knowledgeable and does a lot of detective work, he or she may never be able to find what the spreads were and what he or she actually paid for the markups.

The banks and brokerage firms typically will never disclose what markups they took even if you ask them specific questions. They will tell you these are just normal costs and nothing to be concerned about.

Similar markups (although usually lower) occur in virtually every stock purchase in these portfolios as well. Often, banks and brokerage firms have stocks and bonds in their own inventory or from other customers that they are purchasing on behalf of the consumer in a subsidiary company. They mark up these securities twice without disclosure: once from the subsidiary or other customer to the managing company, and then again to the consumer.

The consumers that are told they are paying around 1 percent are not getting the true picture. In actuality, with all the other hidden fees and markups included with portfolio management usually the combined annual cost is 2 percent or more. However, 2 percent annually is a relative bargain to the actively managed mutual funds, which can exceed 3.5 percent annually.

5.3 Multiple middle men

Inevitably, offshore tax haven investment-portfolio management produces complex trust and brokerage arrangements. The reasons for these complex and expensive structures in offshore tax havens are the lack of efficient financial infrastructure and the demand of the investors to protect their assets.

Brokerage and banking arrangements in tax havens usually are piggybacked onto a large internationally known broker or banker. The offshore investment client would typically open a local brokerage account and then the local broker in the tax haven would open a sub-account in a full-service brokerage in one of the major financial centers around the world (but primarily in the US). These arrangements are necessary because the local brokers just don't have the sophisticated trading platforms to handle large volumes of critical and complex securities transactions.

Island tax havens are sometimes so small they can be literally wiped out by a hurricane or volcano. For example, Montserrat, a Caribbean island, had its capital and airport wiped out by a volcano, so it is no longer considered a tax-haven destination. Numerous other Caribbean islands are damaged by hurricanes quite regularly. If these tax haven islands are not wiped out by a natural disaster, they may be vulnerable to human-created ones such as coups or other political disruptions. If you put a great deal of your assets in these traditional tax havens, what legal recourse would you have to get your assets back if there were a natural disaster or political event? Thus, this creates a need to piggyback offshore arrangements on the more stable financial countries of the world through go-betweens, with each of these middlemen is taking a slice of consumer fees paid directly or indirectly from the portfolio management.

5.4 Asset protection trusts

In traditional tax havens, complex and expensive offshore corporate and trust arrangements are necessary to protect family assets, and to assist families to adjust to the infrastructure deficiencies noted in section **5.3**, as well as for family estate-planning reasons.

There are significant one-time legal and accounting costs to set up offshore trusts or corporations. There are also large annual administration costs to maintain the trusts and corporations.

Each of these go-betweens (i.e., brokers, bankers, trustees, accountants, or advisors) must be paid from the tax haven consumer's pocket. This adds significant one-time and annual costs to using the traditional tax haven.

5.5 Total fees a significant drag

Most people and non-investment-trained advisors underestimate the cost of such high fees on an investment portfolio. For example, a $10 million portfolio of average cost offshore mutual funds could cost 3.5 percent of the total portfolio value, or $350,000 a year in management and trading costs. If the portfolio was earning a relatively good rate of return, for example, 7 percent or $700,000, this 7 percent annual return could not be guaranteed by any portfolio manager but in this current market environment this return could be considered a reasonable average over a number of years. Consequently, 50 percent of the total annual $700,000 portfolio return would be taken in fees, leaving a net return after the management costs of only $350,000 per year. Does this 50 percent skimming off the top of a person's return look like an income tax, particularly for Canadians who are used to paying close to 50 percent of their income to taxes? A person could consider this portfolio expense a hidden tax when comparing a traditional tax haven island to the US, which does have a tax on some but not all kinds of investments. Another example in the next few paragraphs will illustrate why.

Since the US is one of the most highly developed and competitive financial markets in the world, competition keeps the cost of investing down significantly. At my firm, KeatsConnelly, we do not sell investments but we typically recommend US mutual funds or exchange-traded funds that have management expense ratios (MERs) of 0.1 to 0.5 percent, with no significant commissions and loads to purchase or redeem these investments through the client's broker of choice. Compare this with the annual 2 to 3.5 percent MERs and additional fund administration expenses for Canadian and offshore managed funds that also generally come with some sort of significant commission paid by the consumer.

The average American actively managed mutual fund or standard brokerage arrangement has an MER of around 1.5 percent. Large portfolios of individual stocks and bonds with a Registered Investment Advisor (RIA), have management fees around 1 percent. These RIAs, if not associated with a bank or brokerage firm, will manage the spreads or markups on stocks and bonds such that they are minimized and, therefore, insignificant or at least less significant in adding to the total cost of the portfolio.

Comparing the numbers on the $10 million portfolio noted above, we can see that a 0.5 percent annual management expense would be around $50,000. This gives the investment management consumer a net of $650,000 after cost for net investment return. However, because the US has an income tax to get the net spendable return for the investor, this tax must be taken into consideration.

Under current Internal Revenue Service (IRS) rules, the typical tax rate on an investment portfolio would characteristically be less than 20 percent. In this example 20 percent of the $650,000 portfolio after fees, would make the total US income tax bill $130,000, leaving a net-after cost and after-tax return of $520,000. Comparing the $350,000 after-management-cost return in the offshore jurisdiction to the $520,000 after-tax and after-fee return of the more typical US portfolio, the investor could have $170,000 or approximately 50 percent better after-tax and after-investment-management-cost return than the portfolio in the typical island tax haven.

Sample 1 illustrates and compares the standard offshore portfolio arrangement with a more typical US portfolio management and income tax arrangement on this portfolio example. For larger or smaller portfolios, simply move the decimal place so, for example, a $1 million portfolio would typically net $17,000 more after management costs and taxes annually as a resident in the US versus residents of an offshore tax haven.

Often larger portfolios are able to negotiate lower fees in the US or in offshore tax havens. The bottom line is that, as an investor, you certainly can do a lot more as a resident in the US by paying a small amount of tax but having a net average annual income nearly 50 percent, or $170,000 per $10 million invested, which is higher than being a resident in the offshore tax haven with all the additional hidden costs.

The assumption that a portfolio will return 7 percent annually is probably generous based on current market conditions, and can vary greatly depending on the manager and the mix of investments chosen by the manager. I'm not attempting in any manner to provide investment advice in this example or anywhere in this book, I'm only trying to illustrate the impact of fees on a similar $10 million portfolio managed through an offshore jurisdiction versus one managed for a US resident. The consequences of a lower portfolio return than the 7 percent assumed in this example, particularly in the offshore tax haven, means that more of the portfolio return (up to and even exceeding 100 percent of the investment return) is consumed by fees if the portfolio return falls below 3.5 percent. This would not be particularly unusual in today's low-rate environment.

Please note the hidden costs in Sample 1 illustrate only the additional costs for investments in the typical offshore tax-haven arrangement. They do not include the other additional costs discussed in Chapter 2 such as import duties, stamp duties, increased cost of living, and increased travel costs. These additional costs could easily add another $50,000 per year to the offshore traditional tax haven for a person with high net worth, when compared to the US, making the US advantage in this sample in the neighborhood of $220,000 per year or nearly $20,000 per month.

This extra investment cost burden greatly contributes to the hidden tax of traditional tax havens. This major expense is an ongoing income tax equivalent in the so-called tax haven. Most people using traditional tax havens do not even realize they would be better off

Sample 1
PORTFOLIO NET FEES COMPARISON

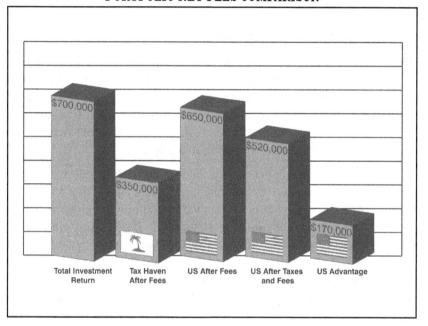

living in the US and paying a small amount of tax but keeping more of their net investment return.

If you can eliminate or reduce investment management costs using US cost-competitive managers and institutions rather than offshore arrangements, with sometimes multiple levels of intermediaries each adding to and taking their cut of the fees, net investment income can be consistently improved.

5.6 No bargains

Many offshore tax-haven clients wrongly assume that because their off-shore broker has opened a sub-bank or brokerage account in the US or Canada they must be getting a good deal. This could not be further from the truth as this typical arrangement is probably the most expensive arrangement the US or Canadian bank or brokerage firm offers the consumer and most often provides no disclosed or undisclosed cost savings operating through a tax haven intermediary or subsidiary. Because they are splitting all commissions, fees, and security spreads and markups with the intermediary, the higher the commissions and undisclosed spreads the more they are able to milk from the offshore tax-haven consumer. This most certainly is not a fair situation in any event if you are a tax-haven consumer of financial services.

5.7 Tax-free options in the US

The US, in addition to having the largest investment choices and trading options in the world, has a substantial number of investment options such as tax-free bonds and tax-deferred annuities. These widely available investment options can be used to eliminate or reduce income taxes on investments for its residents to bring the average tax rate well below the 20 percent used in Sample 1.

If you want to be conservative, and you're a US resident taxpayer, you could zero out the tax on your portfolio by investing in tax-free bonds. These bonds are used to finance the building of airports, roads, bridges, and other municipal infrastructure in the US. Currently, these bonds typically pay 4 to 5 percent (for top-quality credit-rated bonds). The result is if you wish to use the US as your tax haven, you could put your entire portfolio into these bonds and safely earn in the neighborhood of 4 to 5 percent annually, and pay not even five cents of income taxes on the interest earned.

In Chapter 7, I provide the example that Warren Buffett pays approximately 11 percent tax on his income generated through his investments. Consequently, if this lower tax rate could be achieved in Sample 1, the net after-tax and after-cost return in the US could be significantly better than the $170,000 advantage using the US instead of the traditional tax haven.

5.8 Financial leaches

Another hidden cost which manifests in tax havens is a result of the simple fact that traditional tax havens are financial leaches. There are virtually no stocks, bonds, or other investment vehicles directly created in the tax haven. In other words, when a resident living on a traditional tax haven island has an investment portfolio, he or she needs to invest somewhere and those investments are not located in the tax haven. Because those investments are from other countries that actually do have an investment capital creation and maintenance-type financial markets, the typical tax haven financial center is totally dependent on the nontax haven capital markets of the world. As an example, companies such as Apple, Google, or Research in Motion (RIM) were created and are maintained in the US and Canada even though they operate worldwide, and their shares are available in multiple stock exchanges. You will almost never find similar investments that originate in any traditional tax haven.

What does that mean to you, as an investor, who has gone to a tax haven island or center? You are always dealing with a secondary market. It does not matter whether you are buying investments or any other consumer goods and services, the more distance you have between you and the investments, the more people you are paying and, consequently, the more costs you are paying.

The other important factor that results from tax havens not having originated securities is that countries such as Canada and the US have withholding taxes which are charged to offshore investors on their dividends. These withholding taxes are substantially higher for investors located in a tax haven center than for those countries which have treaties with the countries that create the capital markets such as the US and Canada. The withholding tax on dividends from Canadian companies held by foreign investors is 0 to 15 percent with treaty countries but with non-treaty tax havens, the withholding rate is 25 percent. The treaty rate US dividend is 0 to 15 percent for investors from treaty countries and 30 percent, or double, for investors from non-treaty countries and typical tax-haven centers. The tax rate is as low as 5 percent for Canadians living in the US collecting Canadian dividends. Switzerland has 35 percent withholding on dividends and interest on its securities for those living in tax havens, but 0 to 15 percent for those with treaties with Switzerland such as Canada or the US. (See Sample 2.)

The net result is that even though this withholding tax is fully disclosed, it is still one of those costs tax havens have that other more mainstream countries with treaties do not have deal with to the same extent.

5.9 Withholding tax diminishes returns

In a large prudently well-diversified portfolio, withholding taxes on stocks and bonds from various industrialized countries around the world can add up to very significant ongoing costs.

In Sample 3, using the same portfolio and return assumptions as the $10 million portfolio used in Sample 1, the effect of very high rates of withholding on non-treaty tax haven islands becomes clear. Had only

DIVIDEND WITHHOLDING TREATY RATES VERSUS TAX HAVENS

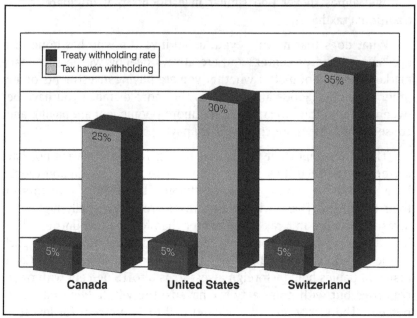

Treaty withholding rate
Tax haven withholding

Canada 5% 25%
United States 5% 30%
Switzerland 5% 35%

half of this portfolio been subject to these withholding taxes from the various industrialized countries around the world (i.e., those noted in Sample 2), averaging 30 percent, the net after-tax and after-fee income available for the tax haven resident to spend could be greatly diminished by this foreign withholding tax. The effect of this withholding tax for the offshore tax-haven investor in Sample 1 is illustrated in Sample 3.

In real numbers the 30 percent withholding on half, or $350,000 of the $700,000 a year income in this sample portfolio, would result in a foreign withholding tax paid of $105,000. Consequently, the total fees of $350,000 and withholding taxes of $105,000 for the offshore portfolio consume a combined total of $455,000 out of $700,000 annually, leaving a net of only $245,000 for the offshore investor to spend each year. The final result would be that this combined $455,000 of the $700,000 total annual return means 65 percent of the portfolio return goes to someone else, rather than the tax-haven investor. In Sample 1, the US investor would have an after-tax and after-fee net income from his or her portfolio of $520,000, or $275,000 more than the $245,000 left for the offshore tax-haven resident. This would put more than $275,000 additional net spendable income per year in a US

Sample 3
PORTFOLIO NET FEES AND TAXES COMPARISON

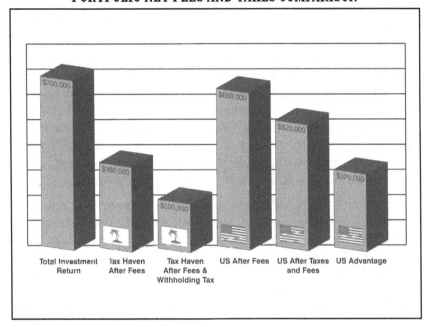

| Total Investment Return | Tax Haven After Fees | Tax Haven After Fees & Withholding Tax | US After Fees | US After Taxes and Fees | US Advantage |

resident investor's pocket annually from the net return on this $10 million portfolio.

In summary, Canadians using the US as their tax haven could have much less than 25 percent of their annual portfolio income consumed by taxes and fees versus 65 percent for those people using a traditional tax haven. Sample 3 shows the enormity of the hidden costs using traditional tax haven residencies.

6. An Example of a Typical Tax Haven Island Family

A very wealthy Canadian family came to KeatsConnelly for assistance in the US. For purposes of confidentiality, we will just call this family the Smiths. They went offshore to the Cayman Islands for all the reasons I have already noted in this and previous chapters, but particularly under the direction of their Canadian accountants and attorneys. This family had children, and when they went offshore, there wasn't any place for these children to go to a quality college once they became of age.

These children became students of US colleges and universities. Two out of three of these children met their spouses in the US, and settled in the US. The third child decided to move back to Canada. This destroyed the family plan faultily constructed by their Canadian advisors to live in the tax haven in the middle of nowhere, ignoring the real dynamics of how to make the plan responsive to the family's lifestyle needs.

Without question, this family would have been better off ignoring their highly paid advisors' advice to go offshore by just moving straight south to the US. The tax saving would have been the same or better than the Cayman Islands and their lifestyle would have fit better with their family needs and desires. However, in this chapter we are temporarily setting aside the priority of lifestyle needs and are only illustrating and concerned with the cost of investment management, as this family had a classical structure for managing their wealth.

The Smith family had several trusts and corporations at one of the major Canadian banks in the Cayman offshore tax center acting as its investment manager and trustee. Their portfolios in the various entities (of which they had at least two for each child and each parent) totaled in the several millions of dollars. When I initially asked the Smith family what it was costing them for this Canadian bank to look after their large investment portfolios, they said it was around 1.5 percent per year — at least that is what they felt was disclosed to them.

However, on further examination, with all the other hidden fees, I noted that the annual cost was in excess of 3 percent. Consequently, it became understandable to them why their portfolio was not growing and producing the kind of income they had expected.

This family has now moved all of their investments to the US at considerable after-tax savings, and some of the family members are now US citizens with their own children born in the US. The Smith family learned the hard way that the path to the lifestyle they wanted could have been much easier and less costly had their advisors not advised them to use an offshore island tax haven. They could have simply gone to the US and saved a lot of family money in the form of lower cost of living, lower portfolio management costs, and lower withholdings on their investments.

Medical Considerations

There are many considerations and concerns for those looking for adequate medical treatment on an offshore tax haven island. Whether routine doctor's visits and medical checkups or major surgeries and treatments, small tax haven countries may have limited choices with unpredictable costs. This chapter will review the very real concerns relating to the extremely important aspects of adequate family medical care in maintaining a desired lifestyle.

Adequate medical plans are generally never discussed by the accountants and lawyers pushing their offshore tax-haven strategies. By ignoring the inevitability that someone in the family will at some time need significant medical treatment while on an offshore island, these advisors inadvertently do a great disservice to Canadians seeking the desired lifestyle of living in a tropical climate. Many families have seen their expensive offshore tax-reduction strategies obliterated by a medical requirement not available on the traditional tax haven island. Can you imagine battling something like breast cancer or prostate cancer from an island in the middle of nowhere, without the support of friends or family, or access to the best doctors and medical facilities in the world? Without good health, nothing else matters, period.

1. Health Insurance Premium Rates

There are many myths about Canadians finding effective and affordable medical insurance when they gain permanent residence in the United States. However, those going to the traditional offshore tax havens have a substantially greater problem in obtaining medical coverage. That never seems to be a concern with the accountants' and lawyers' highly technical and complex offshore plan as there is the underlying assumption that those going to traditional tax havens have sufficient funds to buy individual health insurance or to self-fund the medical costs.

Regardless of how the costs are covered for medical services outside of Canada, these expenses always have to come into the equation because the Canadian medical system is primarily funded through income taxes. Consequently, additional medical costs fall into the category of another hidden tax for Canadians going to a tax haven.

I have designed many medical coverage plans for Canadians, both winter visitors and those becoming permanent US residents. I have also successfully discredited the myth of how difficult and how expensive it is to get coverage in the US. Under new US medical insurance rules, any Canadian moving to the US, as a legal resident, is guaranteed coverage regardless of any preexisting conditions or age. The cost of this coverage is very reasonable considering the possible expenses that may be incurred from the preexisting conditions. Those that have no preexisting conditions have an even greater number of low-cost full-medical options in the US.

The following list includes some sample rates of US health-insurance coverage as of December 2014. This example is for an individual with a preexisting condition in the age range of 55 to 65 in Florida. This does vary from state to state but most of the other states have very similar plans for those individuals with preexisting conditions:

Premium: $682 per month.

Deductible: $0.

This kind of medical insurance coverage is not available for someone with a preexisting condition going to a traditional tax haven or for someone traveling outside of Canada. This means the person is taking a great risk for large medical expenses if he or she has to pay out of his or her own pocket, which could easily exceed any tax savings the person may have by living in a traditional tax haven.

If you don't have a preexisting condition, there are some excellent international health-insurance plans that work to provide full coverage virtually anywhere in the world, including the US and the traditional tax havens, but there is a cost involved. The following list is an example of one of these international medical-insurance plans with a $5,000 deductible (all rates are annual premiums):

- Age 50 to 54: male is $770; female is $859.

- Age 55 to 59: male is $947; female is $955.

- Age 60 to 64: male is $1,640; female is $1,457.

- Age 65 to 69: male is $3,546; female is $3,176.

- Age 70 to 74: male is $5,851; female is $5,240.

These medical insurance costs are not that radically different from some standard Canadian travel insurance rates, yet they cover all 12 months each year and cover all named conditions, not just emergency visits to hospitals outside of Canada. This particular medical insurance coverage is identical for those moving to the US and those moving to traditional tax haven islands. The big difference comes in actually attaining services where there is very little access. Inevitably, tax haven island residents have to travel to gain full access to some of the best doctors, surgeons, and medical facilities in the world, usually by going to the US.

2. Plan Ahead

Obtaining adequate medical coverage is often ignored when a person is taking up residency in a traditional tax haven. A full reconnaissance determining what doctors and what facilities are actually available on the island needs to be completed before taking up residency in one of these countries. Usually, the results of this medical reconnaissance reveal very few medical options, comparatively speaking, to some of the facilities available in major Canadian or US cities.

Those living on a tax haven island usually find themselves taking several plane trips a year just to see their medical specialists or to get adequate medical treatments. For those using the Caribbean tax haven islands that usually means flying to Florida and finding doctors and medical facilities there. If they were already using the US as their tropical lifestyle choice, the travel might be simply hopping in the car and driving down the street to their local doctor or medical facility, which is considerably more convenient, less costly, and less stressful.

Medical emergencies are never fun, regardless of where or when they occur. Easy and immediate access to well-trained emergency room doctors or trauma centers is critical to survival and for the best chance of a full recovery. Getting complete medical treatment in that critical hour after an accident, heart attack, or stroke can mean the difference between full recovery and death or permanent incapacity.

For the more probable emergencies a person may face such as stroke, heart attack, or car accident trauma, unless the person is super wealthy with access to his or her own private doctor, nurse, and private jet, having one of these medical emergencies on an offshore tax haven island can be problematic. How do you get off the island quickly to where you need to be treated, and are you stable enough to fly? A regular ambulance cannot drive you from a Caribbean island to Miami or another US city. These are all factors that become obstacles and highlight the hidden costs of the traditional tax-haven lifestyle.

3. Get the Best Medical Care by Using Both the Canadian and American Systems

When it comes to the ongoing debate as to whether the Canadian or American medical system is better, I find they both have their benefits and disadvantages depending on treatment being sought. I like to show people how they can get the best of both systems - effectively double-dipping.

My 30-plus years of experience in this area has taught me that you can never answer the question in advance as to which of the two medical systems will be best for you, unless you can determine when, where, and what medical assistance you will need in advance. Of course, this is the million-dollar question, because if you knew in advance when, where, and what illness or injury you were going to have, you could research and shop the medical purveyors in either country to get the best care, or work to prevent the problem altogether. However, life never works that way. This is the equivalent of trying to plan your spending in retirement so the last check you write on the day you die bounces! By combining the best benefits from both countries, and planning it so you can double-dip through access to either the Canadian or US medical systems, you can obtain the best protection with the maximum flexibility.

By and large, Canadians leaving Canada lose the provincial health-care plan coverage within 30 to 60 days, depending on the province.

However, to reinstate this coverage, if a person deems it necessary, all he or she needs to do is take up residency once again in the province and 90 days later (residents returning from outside Canada to Alberta, New Brunswick, or Prince Edward Island have no waiting period to become eligible once again), he or she is back on the provincial health-care plan.

In addition, US residents with worldwide coverage insurance policies are covered for medical treatment in Canada, the US, or anywhere else. However, for those Canadians using the US as their personal tax haven, their medical-care options are probably the best medical choices currently available anywhere. These Canadians have access to two of the best medical systems in the world when they need them.

4. Treaty Protection Necessary for Medical Treatment

With the protection afforded by the Canada-US Tax Treaty under the tiebreaker rules outlined in Chapter 5, there is little chance of the taxpayer's tax status being jeopardized due to any necessary extended medical tax treatment administered in Canada or the US. However, if a taxpayer goes to the traditional tax haven offshore, spending necessary extended time in either Canada or the US for medical treatment could subject him or her to full residential tax rates in the country in which he or she receives treatment.

Where the person receives medical treatment is a residential tie, particularly under the Canada Revenue Agency (CRA) rules. If treatment is in Canada, without the treaty protection from the Canada-US Tax Treaty that is provided to US residents, the CRA may attempt to tax the individual as if he or she never left Canada, and collect taxes, interest, and penalties for all income earned since he or she exited the country to go to the traditional tax haven.

The same flexibility and treaty protection is not available to those Canadians going to a traditional tax haven offshore. Hoping the person does not get sick or injured and need medical treatment is not prudent planning. This is how a great traditional tax-haven plan to avoid Canadian taxes may easily be obliterated because of the need or the desire to be treated for necessary medical procedures in Canada or the US. Once more, a person using the US for his or her lifestyle choice and tax haven can be, under normal circumstances, protected by the Canada-US Tax Treaty without fear of adverse Canadian tax consequences.

5. Immigration Concerns for Medical Services

In addition to the tax concerns of getting medical treatment, if you are not a citizen or visa holder of the country in which you are getting treatment, you can have substantial immigration problems if you overstay your visitor visa status because of the length of the treatment.

Many countries will provide special visas for those seeking medical treatment in their respective countries. However, immigration rules are always a hurdle and must be treated with care in order not to violate these rules. It would be extremely critical if Canadian individuals seeking medical treatment originating from residency in a traditional tax haven were refused entry to the US or other foreign country because they had no proper immigration status. Even when visas or waivers are obtained for those Canadians living in traditional tax havens for US medical treatment, visa expiration and time limit concerns create a myriad of technical immigration and tax problems that constantly need to be monitored.

Those people using the US as a tax haven would obviously have some legal immigration status in the US (see Chapter 9) and perhaps would be a dual-Canadian and US citizen with full access at any time either to Canada or the US for any medical situation. This is the maximum freedom of choice that may be lifesaving as well as assist Canadians in maintaining their desired lifestyles with some tax relief.

6. US Medicare Is Available

Canadians older than the age of 65 who resided in the US legally for at least five years, or who are or about to become US citizens, are eligible for complete US Medicare coverage regardless of any preexisting conditions. The minimum cost is approximately $650 per month per person, or $200 per month if the individual or his or her spouse has contributed at least the minimum amount to the US Social Security programs on US employment earnings. Rates can change.

Business persons or business executives using the US as a tax haven can easily qualify for a lower rate for US Medicare by paying themselves or earning a director's fee in excess of $6,000 per year(adjusted for inflation) for up to ten years. This simple act will give them the minimum required number of quarterly credits that the US Social Security administration requires to get the largest part (i.e., Part A) of their US Medicare free. When one spouse gets the minimum number of credits, and both spouses are older than age 65, the other spouse automatically qualifies for the free Medicare Part A coverage as well as a small Social Security pension. For a married couple this is a major benefit because it can reduce their retirement medical expenses after age 65 by about $12,000 per year.

For those persons who do not have any direct-business options or friends with companies from which they can earn paid directors' fees, instead they can earn a minimum $6,000 through a hobby such as creating sellable artwork or working a part-time job. Again, only one spouse needs these minimum employment earnings to obtain the required number of Medicare credits for both spouses to receive free Part A.

Note that there are numerous private insurance carriers that provide recommended Medicare supplements to fill any gaps in the US Medicare coverage.

7. Medical Coverage for Those 75 and Older

For most private health-insurance companies around the world, age 75 is their normal age limit to which they will no longer provide coverage to new applicants. Some companies will cover their customers past age 75 providing they applied before age 75 and are still in good health.

Canadians older than 75 have limited choices for medical insurance outside of Canada. This is particularly true for those with preexisting conditions using traditional tax havens as their residences. Most Canadians know many people older than the age of 75 with preexisting conditions who cannot even get travel insurance to travel outside of Canada under any circumstances from any company.

For people using the US for their tax haven, there are two very good medical insurance options not available to Canadian travelers outside of Canada or those using offshore tax havens for residency:

- US Medicare, available for all those US legal-permanent residents older than 65 who have spent at least five years as US residents, regardless of preexisting conditions. As noted in section 6., those who have contributed to the US Social Security system for the minimum number of earning quarters receive lower premium rates than those who have not contributed.

- The Affordable Care Act, otherwise known as ObamaCare, provides coverage technically at any age with any pre-existing condition to all legal US residents.

Freely being able to enjoy a tropical lifestyle without worry is just as important or even more important for those older than 75. Numerous clients of mine have said to me that the older they get the harder it is to endure Canadian winters, and they would be devastated if they were no longer able to spend the winters in the warm south. Having proper medical insurance coverage ensures them freedom in lifestyle choices. Because of these viable medical-insurance options for those older than 75, using the US as a lifestyle residence of choice once again shows the US is a better alternative than any traditional tax haven.

Lifestyle choices should always be a priority over tax savings. Having the proper medical coverage to ensure freedom of lifestyle choices could mean having US residency would be beneficial even if there were no tax savings or reduction in cost of living.

5

Understanding the Canada-US Tax Treaty

One of the key benefits of using the US for your lifestyle choice for warm climate, lower cost of living, and tax-reduction strategy is that Canada and the US have a very good and well-established tax treaty. The Canada-US Tax Treaty can be the most important tax-planning feature for the protection of a Canadian's financial assets in the US. When dealing with the traditional tax-haven countries that have no treaty with Canada the taxpayer is vulnerable to the whims of the Canada Revenue Agency (CRA), particularly when it comes to the determination of residential ties to Canada.

Under the Canada-US Tax Treaty, the withholding rate on dividends paid by a Canadian company to a foreign individual or corporation can be as low as 5 percent; with a non-treaty country the withholding rate is five times more at 25 percent. There is nothing preventing the CRA from increasing the tax, at any time, on non-treaty country residents beyond 25 percent whereas with the Treaty is extremely difficult to change the rate and it has only changed once in 30 years or more and that was to reduce it from 15 to 5 percent on certain intercompany dividends between Canadian and US companies.

There have been discussions to eliminate the withholding tax entirely for dividends paid from Canada to a US-related company and vice versa. Chapter 6 provides full comparison of nonresident withholding tax rates for all forms of income for people who live in a treaty country (e.g., US) versus a non-treaty country (e.g., traditional tax haven).

1. Tax Treaties Should Be Embraced Rather than Ignored

Most Canadians are completely unaware of the Canada-US Tax Treaty's existence and the benefits that it gives them. Tax planning becomes paramount for Canadians when considering a move abroad.

It is my experience that few financial advisors on either side of the Canada-US border have ever seriously cracked the cover of the Canada-US Tax Treaty on behalf of their clients to look for planning opportunities. Those advisors advising Canadians go to the traditional tax haven think they can ignore treaty benefits available to their clients elsewhere. Accountants, lawyers, and financial planners tend to focus on the domestic tax rules of their own individual countries. Clients risk the backing of proper professional direction of how to exploit the Treaty for their benefits. It is in these clients' best interests to implore their advisors to team up with or refer them to specialists who deal with cross-border tax and other related issues on a regular basis. This will allow clients to properly assess the options of either going offshore to a traditional tax haven or using a treaty such as the Canada-US Tax Treaty.

The Canada-US Tax Treaty is one of the most important tools used in cross-border financial planning to create a tax haven for Canadians in the US for two key reasons:

- The terms of the Treaty take precedence over almost all the *Income Tax Act* (ITA) rules in Canada and the Internal Revenue Code (IRC) tax rules in the US. It is an important trump card to play at appropriate times when doing cross-border planning, particularly when you are doing a major lifestyle change and you want certainty in any tax-reduction strategy to create the ideal tax haven.

- The terms of the Treaty seldom change. In addition, when a change to the treaty is requested by one country or the other there is a protocol that requires substantial communication and negotiation between the tax authorities of both countries. When the changes are agreed to, there is a complex legislative process that requires the treaty changes to be authorized and voted on by the full Parliament in Canada and the US Congress with a Presidential signature.

The Canada-US Tax Treaty, originally established in 1942 during the Second World War, has been amended only six times in its more-than-70-year history, and it can be relied on to a much greater degree for long-term planning than either the Canadian ITA or the American IRC. The ITA and IRC are subject to constant revision without notice and are affected by annual budgets, bipartisan politics, and election campaigns.

Since the last major treaty negotiations in 1989, the IRS has changed the US domestic tax rules an estimated 15,000 times and the CRA has changed its tax rules close to the same amount of times. The 1989 treaty revisions took until 1995 before they were signed into law and the most recent revisions, the Fifth Protocol, started in the year 2000 and were submitted for final approval to the respective federal legislators in 2008. Contrast this somewhat public and lengthy process to change treaty law versus the "behind closed doors" secrecy of the changes that come to domestic tax laws in either Canada or the US, where the politicians dream up new tax rules seemingly overnight and spring them on the public before people have the time to plan or react.

2. Determination of Residency: The Tiebreaker

One of the foremost roles of the Canada-US Tax Treaty is its tiebreaker rules for determination of residency. These rules prevent a situation where an individual is taxed as a resident of Canada and the US at the same time on their worldwide income. Being taxable on worldwide income in two countries at the same time would inevitably mean a taxpayer would pay tax twice on the same or similar income.

Through treaty law, which overrides the myriad domestic rules pertaining to residency from both the CRA and the IRS, the Treaty states that an individual is only required to pay tax on his or her worldwide income in either Canada or the US, but not both countries. This treaty law is critical and very useful in enabling Canadians to use the US as their choice for tax haven.

By following the Canada-US Tax Treaty four tiebreaker rules listed below, and passing just one of the four successive tests clearly in favor of one or the other country, the taxpayer will be protected from having to face two complete sets of tax rules at the same time and prevent double taxation on certain forms of income. The tiebreaker rules, in Article IV of the Canada-US Tax Treaty, are outlined here, along with comments to explain them:

1. *The individual shall be deemed to be a resident of the country in which he or she has a permanent home available. If a permanent home is available in both countries, or neither, an individual is deemed to be resident in the country in which his or her personal and economic relations are closer (center of vital interests).*

Generally, a "permanent home" is any accommodation that is considered permanent. The home may be rented or owned. It is considered permanent where it is available for the individual's use throughout the year. A large summer lake cottage in Canada not designed for or available for use throughout the winter would not be considered a permanent home whereas a small condominium in a city would be. When a person has a permanent home in both Canada and the US, it is generally better, but not mandatory, to have the larger home in your desired country of residence. A person's center of vital interests would be objectively determined and would be based upon his or her familial, social, occupational, political, and cultural activities. Economic relations are also considered and are generally linked with the locality of the primary sources of income.

2. *If the country in which the individual has his or her center of vital interests cannot be decisively determined, he or she shall be determined to be a resident of the country in which he or she has an habitual abode.*

The "center of vital interest" is generally interpreted as an economic center as to where the taxpayer derives his or her primary sources of income, particularly those sources of income in which he or she has flexibility of choice. For example, if a person was living off income from his or her investment portfolio, it generally can be moved voluntarily to his or her country of chosen residency. The location of the investment portfolio would likely be considered a vital interest for treaty-residency determination. Whereas, if he or she was receiving a pension (e.g., Canada Pension), the beneficiary of that pension has no choice in the matter to relocate the pension source. For a US resident, since that Canada pension income must come from Canada, the source of the pension would not be considered a vital interest for the determination of residency.

What constitutes "habitual abode" requires an evaluation of the individual's lifestyle over a sufficient length of time. In most circumstances, the length of time spent and where a spouse and/or any minor dependent children are normally located in one country over another may be determinative under this test. In addition, the transient nature of the stay may be examined (e.g., living at a seasonal vacation cabin at the lake for a few summer months versus six months or more at a typical year-round residence in the city).

3. *If the individual has a habitual abode in both countries or in neither country, he or she shall be deemed to be resident of the country of which he or she is a citizen.*

The immigration status is very important; for example, if a person was to have a permanent residence status, that would most definitely be considered as to whether he or she had a habitual abode for the purposes of determining residency under the Treaty. It would be very difficult, if not impossible, for a Canadian to use the treaty to become a US resident if he or she has no legal immigration status of any form in the US. Ultimately, citizenship is the final determination if none of the first two tests are determinative.

4. *If the individual is a citizen of both countries (generally the most recent citizenship obtained will be considered the primary citizenship barring other dominant factors), or of neither of them, then competent authorities of the contracting countries shall settle the question by mutual agreement.*

The "competent authorities" are committees of individuals from both Canada and the US who examine the facts and make a determination. This process should be avoided at all costs, as it is lengthy, costly, and heart-wrenching. It is difficult to determine in advance what the outcome of the competent authority committee may be. It is not a formal legal process with a judge and jury; it is just a small group of selected individuals reviewing the facts as presented with a certain amount of negotiations back and forth.

2.1 Choice and control of residency

An examination of the Treaty tiebreaker rules in the previous section clearly shows individuals have power over, and can arrange their affairs to maintain control of every single aspect of these tiebreaker rules. This means individuals have as much control as needed to make the determination of residency in favor of the country in which they would prefer to be taxed and protected under the Treaty from double taxation. Individuals only need to pass the first test as to where they have a permanent home so the other three tiebreaker rules after this first rule become moot or at least not significant. If one wishes to keep the family home or any home in Canada when they become a resident of the US under the Treaty there are numerous planning options and can be used. For example, one could place their home in a simple cross-border trust with the children as beneficiaries and a leaseback agreement to lease the home for only a few days, weeks or months each year. The rent paid by the parents could offset any of the expenses of running the home such as utilities maintenance and property taxes make these expenses deductible to get some tax advantages from this arrangement.

I never recommend those wishing to use the US as their lifestyle choice and tax haven to rely on only the first of the tiebreaker rules. I would generally recommend individuals make certain, to the extent they have control, to ensure they pass the principal residence, the center of vital interest, and the habitual abode tiebreaker tests simultaneously. If possible, and the proper immigration credentials are available, I would also recommend them to become dual citizens of Canada and the US. Though not officially mentioned in these first three tiebreaker rules, immigration status sneaks into the determination of vital interest and habitual abode because in order to be a nonresident of Canada they need to have legal residency in the US. The CRA will, if individuals have no legal status in the US, assuredly have a valid justification to say the taxpayers never left Canada and tax them accordingly for the income they earned since they left Canada and stopped paying taxes on their worldwide income in Canada.

2.2 Breaking Canadian ties for a traditional tax haven island

Although the Treaty tiebreaker rules as discussed in the previous sections can be a bit confusing, they are relatively easy to follow to ensure a taxpayer receives the desired outcome. However, anyone moving to a traditional tax haven island has only the CRA's domestic rules, which are more complicated and difficult to overcome. These CRA rules dictate very clearly that just about anything you do or leave in Canada is considered a residential tie and subjects you to tax on your worldwide income in Canada.

To become a nonresident with no Treaty protection you need to sell or move every asset you own in Canada, and close all bank accounts, investment accounts, RRSPs, etc., before you move to the traditional tax haven. Something as simple as leaving a piece of furniture, a vehicle, or a boat in Canada shows you have intent to return and, therefore, you have not broken residential ties.

Most advisors recommend if you are going to exit Canada to a traditional tax haven, that you not even visit Canada for at least two years after you have broken every possible residential tie with Canada. Any visits after the first two years should be of a very short duration and not all that frequent. It is my personal belief this is a great sacrifice for close families and those who have a very active social network of friends. Weddings, reunions, funerals, birthdays, bar mitzvahs, and get-togethers will all suffer greatly. Lifestyle and family relationships should take priority over tax savings.

If you are using the US as your lifestyle choice and tax haven, you will face few of these same restrictions. Providing you follow one or more of the easy-to-follow tiebreaker rules over which you have full control, US Treaty residents can visit Canada regularly, own a business in Canada, and keep a secondary residence, a vehicle, a boat, etc., in Canada without fear of the CRA trumping the Canada-US Tax Treaty residency rules.

3. The Treaty Allows You to Run a Business in Canada from the US

If you are a semi-retired person who has a Canadian business that no longer requires that you be present on a daily basis in Canada, you then have the complete flexibility operate your business from the US side of the border. Consequently, you can easily control most of the factors discussed in section 2's Treaty tiebreaker rules. If you are a creative business owner, you can devise a very simple and effective way to run the business by remote control by doing most of your work while in the US by telephone, fax, video conferencing, and email. You would be considered a US resident under most of the tiebreaker rules including habitual abode and center of vital interest tiebreaker rules. In effect, you can control in which country you are taxed on your worldwide income.

We had a client who lived a very comfortable lifestyle in Palm Springs while running his manufacturing business located in British Columbia literally on a daily basis with remote control video cameras. His office, in his large Palm Springs home, looked like a NASA control center with all the video screens tied to the Canada business cameras. He only traveled back to Vancouver once a year for the company Christmas party!

These Treaty tiebreaker rules work extremely well to protect the family-owned business where the parents want to retire in the US Sun Belt and let the children run the business on a day-to-day basis in Canada. If the children run the business into the ground, the parents can still be in control of the business and can easily do so from the US, travelling to Canada to help out as necessary.

Farmers who wish to pass their farm on to their children can return from their US residences each spring and fall to help with the spring planting and the fall harvest, and leave the children to run the farm the rest of the year.

There are some great tax strategies discussed in Chapter 7 that allow parents to gradually sell or transfer their businesses or farms to their children at extremely low treaty tax rates. Often the tax due on selling a business to family members is so onerous that parts of the business need to be sold to strangers just to pay the taxes. Usually, the cross-border strategy will reduce the taxes to the effect that if there are taxes to be paid, they can be paid out of cash flow and the business is maintained in its entirety to grow and prosper for the next generation.

Running a Canadian business from a traditional tax haven without the protection of the Treaty tiebreaker rules would almost certainly end up in a long, painful, and losing tax battle with the CRA. The business ownership and the needs of the business would be a huge red flag of residential ties to Canada and, therefore, obliterate any tax reduction plans through a tax haven other than under the Canadian Treaty umbrella with the US.

If you are in the occupation of a consultant or computer programmer who can readily work anywhere, your center of vital interest can move with you to the US quite easily even though some or all of your customers are still in Canada.

4. No Need to Drop Your Canadian Directorships

If you are retired but you still sit on one or more board of directors in Canada, you can continue to remain on these boards when you move to the US.

Generally, there is no need to be concerned as to whether your center of vital interest would be determined to remain in Canada if the other tiebreaker rules were followed closely to make you a treaty resident of the US.

Sitting on boards of Canadian corporations can be a great lifestyle choice for retired executives as they can keep their finger in the business world they have known their entire careers yet have the freedom to travel and enjoy the lifestyle they have worked hard to achieve. This would be nearly impossible to do from a traditional tax haven island but it is easy to do and done very regularly by many executives from their US home base. Often, many Canadian board meetings happen in the US in the areas that Canadians using the US as a tax haven would normally reside such as Palm Springs, Palm Beach, or Phoenix. This makes travel to and from board meetings very convenient with numerous transportation alternatives including driving.

5. Bronfman Rules

In the early 1990s, the Bronfman family legally took several billions of dollars of the Seagram Company's stock with them when they moved to the US without paying any Canadian tax on the unrealized capital gains on this stock. Canada Revenue Agency (CRA), or Revenue Canada as it was called at that time, considered this a loophole after the fact. In an attempt to plug this perceived loophole, the CRA developed a new set of rules to prevent this from happening again with other Canadian taxpayers. These specifically created rules are commonly known as the Bronfman rules.

One part of the Bronfman rules was designed by the CRA to prevent Canadians that had been using Canadian domestic tax rules to remain Canadian residents while at the same time using the Canada-US Tax Treaty to become a taxpayer of the US. This little convenient arbitrage of the laws would allow Canadians to become treaty residents of the US to take advantage of the lower US tax rates without going through the deemed disposition or exit tax leaving Canada. Avoiding the exit or departure tax would be of great advantage to the taxpayer but very problematic with the CRA.

The CRA amended the Canadian *Income Tax Act*. The amendment the CRA added to the Act was Section 250 (5). To paraphrase this new act: Under the Canada-US Tax Treaty, if a taxpayer is a resident of the US (or any other treaty country), he or she is automatically a nonresident taxpayer of Canada. This new residency rule certainly achieved the results CRA was looking for which was to force Canadians through an exit process and to pay exit tax before they could enjoy the lower treaty rates of the US. On the surface, this all sounds very bad but in actuality, it is a very useful rule that assists Canadians using the US as their tax haven.

The major side benefit provided by this new rule of Section 250 (5) to Canadians living in the US is they no longer have to deal with Canadian domestic residency rules being used against them. The Treaty tiebreaker residency rules trump the CRA domestic rules. Without the Treaty residency rules, the domestic residency rules could be used by the CRA to tax US residents on their world income because they left some minor financial ties with Canada when they exited, or spent significant time in Canada after their exit. Now, thanks to the Bronfman rules, as long as Canadians follow the provisions of the tiebreaker rules in the Treaty, they can have full confidence that the lower Treaty tax rates and the lower US tax rates will be applicable versus the higher Canadian rates.

5.1 Don't wave red flags at the CRA

It is never prudent to waive a red flag at the CRA by maintaining significant Canadian ties after a tax exit from Canada even when moving to the US.

However, Section 250 (5) of the Canadian *Income Tax Act* means Canadians taking up US residency could, for example, maintain a Canadian cottage, residence, vehicle, or spend reasonable visiting time (even as much as six months) in Canada annually. Provided the taxpayers followed the Treaty tiebreaker rules for all the major items that count in determining the country in which they are a tax resident, the CRA, by its own rule, cannot tax them on their worldwide income.

This Section 250 (5) provision of the *Income Tax Act* does not apply to Canadians using the traditional tax haven countries. As mentioned earlier, most advisors would suggest to those going offshore to a traditional tax haven from Canada that they do not return to Canada at all during the first two years unless it is for a funeral or some major family event. In addition, someone going to a traditional tax haven should cut all other residential ties with Canada such as close all bank investment accounts, sell principal residences, sell automobiles, and sell furniture so as not to leave any personal items in Canada that might indicate intention to return.

The CRA has been successful, on numerous occasions, in determining individuals going to non-tax treaty countries were residents of Canada and that they never left for tax purposes. Such simple items such as leaving a vehicle in a relative's garage, leaving some furniture in storage, keeping an RRSP investment in Canada, or any other seemingly innocent similar residential ties have all been used by the CRA to claim residential ties and, therefore, to tax persons caught under these rules as full Canadian residents. Much to the chagrin and financial downfall of these taxpayers, they had to fight the CRA to try to prevent them from being taxed on their entire income since they left Canada and lost under the Canadian domestic residency rules.

The protection afforded by the Canada-US Tax Treaty in combination with the CRA's own rule, Section 250 (5), takes away the CRA's power to use these minor residential ties as an excuse to collect taxes it has no right to collect. This powerful combination of treaty and Canadian domestic rules allows those who use the US as their tax haven to sleep comfortably and travel back and forth to Canada easily and as frequently as they desire without having to look over their shoulder to see whether the CRA tax man is coming after them!

6. The Tax Treaty Prevents Double Taxation

The Treaty tiebreaker rules are not enough to give complete protection to Canadians wanting full tax haven status in the US. Taxpayers must also use the second major benefit of the Canada-US Tax Treaty, which is to prevent Treaty protected taxpayers from being double taxed on all sources of income created in either of the two countries.

Double tax does not necessarily mean the tax is exactly double. Double tax is defined as paying tax in one country without getting any further credit and paying tax again in another country. This means that the taxpayer is paying at least one level more of taxes between the two countries than he or she needs to so, in effect, paying a double tax.

Often, businesses that fail to plan properly for cross-border transactions are subjected to three levels of tax; two more levels of tax than are necessary.

The treaty prevents double tax in three key ways: foreign tax credits, exemptions, and withholding rates, which are discussed in the following sections.

6.1 Foreign tax credits

The Treaty allows for a system of credits so that tax paid to one country on specified income will be allowed as a full credit against any tax due on that same income in the other country or country of residence. For example, a nonresident who earns a taxable rental income in Canada files and pays tax as required by the CRA using a nonresident Canadian tax return. The tax paid to the CRA after netting income and expenses on a nonresident T1 tax return (under Section 216 of the Canadian *Income Tax Act*) is converted to US funds, adjusted for US depreciation and rental expense rules, and is used on the US return as a full foreign tax credit. This reduces the US income tax on Canadian rental income by the amount of the credit, or eliminates US taxes altogether if the credit from the Canadian filing is larger than the tax due to the IRS on this Canadian rental income.

In the majority of situations, Canadian tax is higher than US tax due on identical income, creating a surplus of foreign tax credits for the US taxpayer. The IRS has generous tax credit rules, which allows any unused credits that are surplus from the current year to be carried forward for up to ten additional years. Consequently, the taxpayer may have credits to be used against future foreign income earned even if it is from a different country and a different type of investment income than where the credits were originally generated. Following through on this Canadian rental income example, if the CRA collected $1,000 tax on this rental income and the IRS tax rates were such that the US taxpayer only had $500 tax due to the IRS on exactly the same rental income, this would mean that the taxpayer would have a surplus of $500 of foreign tax credits to carry forward to use to reduce taxes for up to ten years or until the credits are used up on future foreign income. This is a very simple but very powerful planning tool for Canadians using the US as a tax haven.

The CRA is not as generous and limits these foreign tax credits for Canadian residents to the amount of the stated Canada-US Tax Treaty withholding rates on any specific taxable income source, regardless of what foreign tax was actually paid. The IRS allows full foreign credits for actual tax paid, a very important benefit for those using the US as a tax haven because it provides the flexibility to allocate surplus credits and many other controllable sources of foreign income, greatly reducing US taxes payable.

Normally, Canadians going to a non-treaty traditional tax haven would not need to use foreign tax credits, because there is generally no tax due in the tax haven on residual Canadian income while living in the tax haven. However, as noted in Chapters 3 and 6, the withholding rate from the CRA is much higher than with the treaty rate when the taxpayer is a US resident.

The CRA will not give credit for taxes paid in a traditional offshore tax haven arrangement. With no treaty protection, taxpayers using a traditional tax haven are often very vulnerable if they inadvertently left residential ties in Canada. They could lose the battle with the CRA and have the CRA collecting taxes for the entire time since they left the country for the tax haven. This could mean that combined with the non-treaty withholding tax rates on Canadian-sourced income, and with the regular Canadian income tax the CRA would normally collect from residents, the total reassessed tax, interest, and penalties could be as high as 100 percent of the income generated in the years in question. This is potential disaster for those using the traditional tax haven without the Treaty protection provided to those going to the US.

6.2 Exemptions

The Canada-US Tax Treaty provides for certain exemptions from filing or reporting income of a nonresident in Canada that would otherwise be taxable by the CRA. There is a Treaty provision that allows Canadians in the US to earn up to $10,000 annually in Canada through employment without being taxed in Canada on that income. For example, for someone sitting on a board of directors which had four meetings a year in Canada and paid a director's fee of $2,500 per meeting, he or she would owe no taxes to the CRA on this income. As a US taxpayer, this director would only pay the lower US rates on this income and perhaps no tax at all if he or she had foreign tax credits available from other sources.

With the latest Treaty protocol, interest earned in Canada by residents of the US is exempt from withholding. There are no exemptions for Canadians using traditional tax havens; full nonresident withholding tax would be owed on any residual income earned in Canada (see Chapter 6 for more details).

6.3 Withholding rates

Provisions in the Treaty establish the amount of maximum withholding tax either country can take on various forms of income in that country from residents of the other country. The provisions for maximum withholding rates prove very useful when doing cross-border planning.

The withholding tax rates are explained in more detail in Chapter 6, but are summarized here:

- 15 percent on dividends (5 percent on dividends between related companies).

- 15 percent on periodic withdrawals from Canadian registered plans (i.e., RRSPs, RRIFs, RCAs, IPPs, LIRAs) or the equivalent US plans.
- Zero percent on CPP, QPP, OAS, and US Social Security.
- Zero percent on interest not connected with a trade or business.
- Zero percent on capital gains other than gains on real property. Withholding taxes on gains on real property are determined by the respective domestic rules of each country.
- 15 percent on pension income.
- 25 percent on gross rental income (most taxpayers can reduce this withholding amount to the net taxable rental income by filing nonresident tax returns).

7. Treaty Tax Rates Are Less than Tax Haven Tax Rates

The Canada-US Tax Treaty can be used to reduce the level of taxes on residual Canadian income for Canadians living in the US, to levels well below those of traditional tax havens. For example, if you have a Canadian pension or large RRSPs or RRIFs (or any other Canadian registered plans), the Treaty withholding rate for Canadians living in the US for the periodic payments is only 15 percent, whereas in a tax haven without the benefit of the treaty the withholding rate would be 25 percent. Consequently, the Treaty withholding rate is 10 percent less in the US than in the traditional tax haven.

The Treaty rate for Canadian dividends collected in the US is 15 percent whereas the non-treaty rate is 25 percent. The Treaty rate for Canadian rental income is 25 percent versus 50 percent for the non-treaty rate. Consequently, for someone who has these sources of income, without any great deal of planning and by moving a few miles to the south across the 49th parallel he or she can cut his or her income taxes substantially.

However, with planning, someone with a large RRSP can not only reduce his or her taxes from, say, 50 percent in Quebec and Nova Scotia to the Treaty rate of 15 percent for periodic withdrawals (25 percent on lump-sum withdrawals), a substantial reduction in taxes by itself, he or she also has the opportunity to recover the total taxes withheld by the CRA through foreign tax credits. As noted earlier, the IRS has a very generous foreign tax credit recovery set of rules. When applied correctly to RRSP withdrawals, an even lower effective net tax rate, or in many cases a zero net tax rate on the withdrawal of the RRSP can be realized from the US side of the border. To reduce the tax rate on RRSPs or other Canadian registered plans to as close to a net of zero as possible requires the planning of a skilled cross-border financial planner and is not a do-it-yourself project. The tax savings can be tremendous, particularly if the taxpayer is one of the fortunate Canadians with a seven-figure RRSP. Chapter 8 discusses RRSPs and similar registered plans in more detail.

6

Receiving Income While Living in a Tax Haven

The previous chapters dealt largely with some key lifestyle concerns and tax considerations but this chapter will discuss the important topic of income. This includes all types of income that someone can expect to earn from almost any type of employment, business, real estate, or portfolio of investments.

This chapter will also give a comparison of the three distinctly different tax jurisdictions focused on in this book - Canada, the United States, and the traditional tax haven. I clearly show specific examples of what this means to Canadians looking for tax relief, big or small. I expand on the many different levels of income and types of income, so you can see the real picture in order to make the right choice for the best tax haven if tax relief is something that you want to fit in with your lifestyle choices. As noted in the earlier chapters, I firmly believe that lifestyle choices should be driving factor in choosing a diversion from Canadian winters, with tax savings and potential lower cost of living as secondary factors.

In this chapter, each type of income will be addressed separately. By isolating each type of income, you will be able to determine from your own personal circumstances how these examples may or may not apply to your specific types of income. Most people will have to combine multiple sources of income to make a proper assessment.

Towards the end of this chapter, in section **15**, there are real examples to help you understand the combined effect of different income sources, for a more clear contrast. These examples include high and average income levels of individuals and couples who also have multiple sources of income types.

An example of this "by income type" comparison is the Canadian taxpayer couple, Tim and Tara, who are both in the highest Canadian tax brackets. Tim and Tara would like to know what additional taxes they would pay if one, or both of them, earned another $100,000 of income from their investments or some other income sources. They would like to understand the difference between the US as a tax haven or a traditional tax haven, versus what they would pay if they stayed in Canada on this exact same income. To illustrate this to readers as clearly as possible, I have used $100,000 for each of the different kinds of income to pay as well the annual maximum of the Canada Pension Plan (CPP) and Old Age Security (OAS).

Although this by-income-type method of comparing taxes does not necessarily work in the real world, it certainly is very useful as it illustrates the general trends, and assists in planning when individuals have choices in the type of income they can manufacture or control. For example, investors can focus on either interest or dividends from an investment portfolio depending on which works best for them. Exact tax calculations along with illustrative sample charts are included in the myriad examples after this first section with each of the income types discussed separately.

The baseline assumptions for Tim and Tara by income type with comparisons are the following:

- The combined provincial and federal Canadian tax rates are 50 percent for both Tim and Tara (Ontario, New Brunswick, PEI, Nova Scotia and Quebec are currently at or near this tax level while most other provinces are not far behind).

- Since both Tim and Tara are in the maximum tax brackets, Canadian income-splitting benefits are not available but would be available in the US because they would normally be filing their US return as a married couple filing a joint return.

- The US state of residence for purposes of the comparison for Tim and Tara is Florida.

- Tim and Tara each have RRSPs, and therefore may use the withholding tax from withdrawing their RRSPs as US residents to help them reduce taxes on their future qualified investment income in the US.

- On their income level in the US, their $100,000 of each of the separate income types would be taxed at a high of 30 percent. (A married couple in Florida does not even enter the current maximum tax bracket of 39.6 percent until after their total taxable income, after all deductions and reductions exceeds approximately $500,000 CAD.)

1. Interest Income

As a Canadian resident, Tim, in the 50 percent bracket, would pay $50,000 income tax on an additional $100,000 of interest income from Canadian term deposits, Guaranteed Investment Certificates (GICs), and bonds. If Tim and Tara went to the traditional tax haven and they maintained the same interest-bearing investments, their tax would be reduced to $0. If they were US residents, the CRA also would not withhold any tax on this interest income and Tim's Canadian tax would be zero. The amount of US tax they might have to pay would be $30,000 without credits but since, under the assumptions noted earlier, they have foreign tax credits from withdrawing their RRSPs, the US net tax is zero.

Tim and Tara would save $50,000 annually using the US as their place of residence. (Note that if Tim and Tara had no foreign tax credits available to offset US tax on their interest income they could convert to tax-free municipal bonds in any amount or extent appropriate and still have zero tax due in the US.) See Sample 4.

2. US Corporate Dividend Income

For Tim and Tara, earning $100,000 of non-Canadian or US dividend income, they pay Canadian tax identical to earning $100,000 interest income in Sample 4; in other words, they would pay the regular Canadian tax of $50,000.

Living on a traditional tax haven island, Tim and Tara would pay $30,000 of US nonresident withholding tax on this dividend. If Tim and Tara were residents of the US, they would pay only $15,000 of income tax on this same $100,000 of US corporate dividends. The advantage for Tim and Tara again goes to the US in the amount of $15,000 annually over the traditional tax haven and $35,000 better than the tax Tim and Tara would pay as residents of Canada. It should be noted

Tax on $100,000 Interest Income Comparison

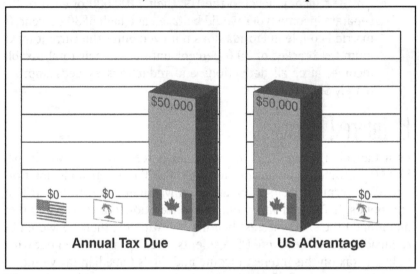

that under the new tax rates introduced by President Obama to cover ObamaCare subsidies that if Tim and Tara's taxable income exceeded approximately $300,000 CAD the tax rate on US dividends could be as high as 23.8 percent on dividends over this threshold. The assumptions used here are the Tim and Tara are right on this threshold so substantially all their dividends would be taxed at the 15 percent rate. See Sample 5.

3. Canadian Qualified Dividend Income

Canadian dividends, both eligible (i.e., dividends from corporations that pay the regular corporate tax rates) and non-eligible (i.e., dividends from private Canadian corporations that distribute income on which they paid the reduced small-business tax rates) are provided favorable tax rates through a system of tax credits to adjust for the fact that the corporations have already paid tax on that specific income.

For Tim and Tara, they would pay approximately $35,000 in Canada on their $100,000 of eligible Canadian dividends. As residents of a traditional tax haven, they would pay a nonresident Canadian withholding tax of 25 percent for a total of $25,000 in taxes. If they were using the US as their tax haven, the tax bill on this income would be $15,000. Again, the advantage goes to the US, a $10,000 tax reduction on the

Sample 5
$100,000 US Dividend Income Comparison

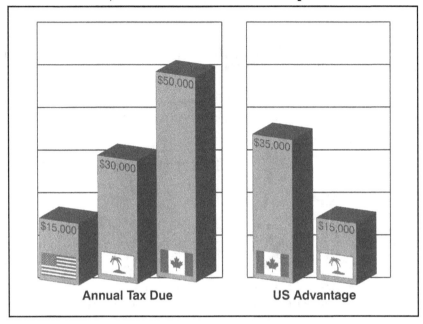

Annual Tax Due	US Advantage

eligible dividends over the traditional tax haven and a $20,000 reduction on the same Canadian dividends as US residents. See Sample 6.

4. Canadian Real Estate Capital Gains

Most Canadians, including Tim and Tara, would like to enjoy the lifestyle such that they could maintain some form of residence in Canada. However, keeping personal real estate in Canada when they go to a traditional tax haven is not recommended because it could be considered a residential tie and subjects them to taxes on their worldwide income in Canada. For those going to the US, they can leave some residential ties as long as they follow the Treaty tiebreaker rules noted in Chapter 5.

If Tim and Tara have a property they wish to sell (as nonresidents of Canada this property would not qualify for the principal residence tax exemption), and they have a $100,000 capital gain, the tax they would pay in Canada on this gain as Canadian residents would be $25,000. If they were residents of a traditional tax haven, or if they were using the US as a tax haven, the tax would be the same because real property is taxed according to the rules of the country in which the real estate is

Tax on $100,000 Canadian Dividend Income Comparison

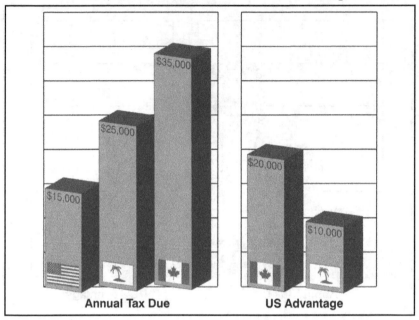

located at the domestic rates, regardless of who owns it or how it's owned. However, the US tax on the gain would only be $15,000 when Tim and Tara filed with the US tax return and the $25,000 payment to Canada would provide a surplus of $10,000 in tax credits that could be used to reduce income taxes on the other foreign income (e.g., interest income on Canadian bonds or GICs). The US has the advantage over both the traditional tax haven and the Canadian resident income tax by the $10,000 tax credit. See Sample 7.

5. General, Non-Real Estate Capital Gains

Regular capital gains, like those earned by selling a stock or other investment that had appreciation attract the same rate of tax as Canadian residents, so Tim and Tara would pay the same $25,000 as they paid in section 4. for Canadian real estate capital gains. However, if they were resident in the traditional tax haven, they would have no tax to pay on this gain.

If they were US residents, they would have a tax due of $15,000. Once again, if they had a surplus of foreign tax credits and they developed

Sample 7
Tax on $100,000 Canadian Real Estate Capital Gains
Income Comparison

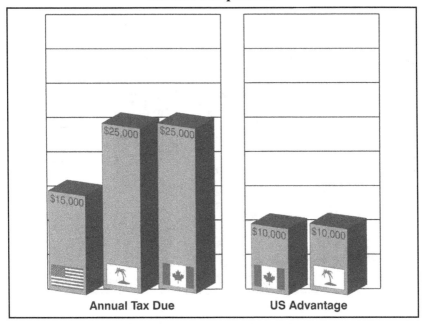

| Annual Tax Due | US Advantage |

the proper investment structure that, under IRS rules, classified this capital gain as a foreign capital gain, foreign tax credits could be used to reduce the tax on this gain in the US to zero for relative savings of $25,000. (If there were no foreign tax credits available for use on the US tax return, Tim and Tara would pay the $15,000 US income tax out of pocket rather than out of the foreign tax credit surplus and would have only $10,000 of savings over Canada rather than $25,000 noted in Sample 8.)

In this case there is no advantage in comparing the US residency to the tax haven but there is still $25,000 in potential savings for Tim and Tara over their regular Canadian capital gains tax. See Sample 8.

6. Pension and Annuities

If Tim or Tara added $100,000 pension income, as Canadian taxpayers, they would pay the maximum tax rate of $50,000 on this income. If they were living on one of the traditional tax haven islands, they

Tax on $100,000 Capital Gains Income Comparison

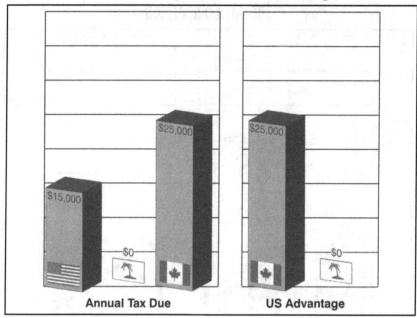

Annual Tax Due	US Advantage

would pay $25,000 in Canadian nonresident withholding tax on this pension. If they were using the US as their tax haven, they would pay a nonresident withholding tax of only $15,000 at the Canada-US Tax Treaty rates.

Since we are assuming Tim and Tara would be filing a joint return in the US with a US tax rate of 30 percent, the tax on the $100,000 of pension in the US would be $30,000 before foreign tax credits are taken. However, since there is at least $15,000 of foreign tax credits directly available from the Canadian nonresident withholding rate, their US tax would be a net of $15,000. The net US tax could be as low as zero dollars if there are foreign tax credits available in addition to the $15,000 that Canada collected under the treaty.

If we assume that Tim and Tara did the proper planning with surplus foreign tax credits, the advantage of the US over the traditional tax haven on the $100,000 of pension income is $10,000 and $35,000 annually over the tax rate they would have to pay as Canadian residents on the pension. (If there were no surplus foreign tax credits available, they would only have an advantage in the US of a $20,000 tax reduction as Canadian residents and they would pay $5,000 more in taxes as US residents than as residents of a traditional tax haven.)

Annuities for nearly all tax purposes work exactly the same as pensions, unless the annuity was purchased with after-tax dollars rather than through a Canadian registered plan. If the annuity was purchased with after-tax dollars, the nonresident withholding tax that CRA takes would only be on the interest earnings part of the annuity, not the principal, so the tax haven advantage still remains with the US for both pensions and annuities. See Sample 9.

7. Periodic Registered Plan Withdrawals

Periodic withdrawals from almost any form of Canadian registered plans are taxed in a similar manner to pensions under the Canada-US Tax Treaty for US residents. Periodic withdrawals are defined as equal payments not exceeding 10 percent so that, in theory, the payments are spread over no less than ten years. The US has the better advantage for Canadians once more, in a manner similar to the pensions in section 6.

If Tim and Tara were to move to a traditional tax haven, the nonresident withholding tax paid to the CRA would increase from 15 to 25 percent, or about two thirds more.

One major additional benefit that can be achieved by Canadians moving to the US versus a traditional tax haven is that the IRS will recognize that, under US domestic rules, these registered plans have a cost basis. What that means to a couple such as Tim and Tara is that only a portion of the $100,000 income from these registered plans will be taxable in the US. For example, if Tim and Tara properly planned before moving to the US, they would have sold all of their securities in their RRSP and left the cash in the RRSP. Their US cost basis would be equal to whatever the full market value of the RRSP funds was when they crossed the border to take up residency in the US. Whatever that value was on the date of exit from Canada, that cost basis may be withdrawn tax-free from the US. The foreign tax credits withheld by the CRA at the 15 percent rate would be available to use for other purposes and to carry forward for as many years (up to ten) that it would take to use all of the credits.

I have given many examples of where these credits can come in handy with the reminder that these credits are like gold; they reduce taxes due by one dollar for each and every dollar of foreign tax credit

Sample 9
Tax on $100,000 Pension Income Comparison

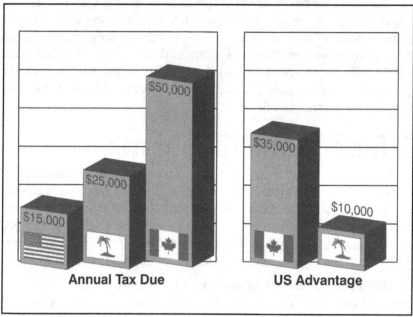

available. The advantage for Tim and Tara using the US as a tax haven with RRSP or RRIF periodic withdrawals can be as high as $50,000 annually over the normal Canadian tax rates, and $25,000 more than the traditional tax haven taxes. See Sample 10.

8. Lump-Sum Withdrawals from RRSPs

Lump-sum RRSP-type withdrawals for Tim and Tara for most purposes, once they are nonresidents of Canada, are similar to the periodic withdrawals mentioned in section **7.**, including the cost basis advantage if they become US residents. The key exception is that the withholding rate that the CRA takes on lump sums is the same whether Tim and Tara are residents of a traditional tax haven or the US.

With proper planning, RRSPs can be a big advantage to those individuals that make the lifestyle choice to live in the US, as they are great foreign tax credit generators and those surplus foreign tax credits can be used to reduce US taxes on other forms of investment income. Because RRSPs are a very large part of Canadians' net worth, and they can

Tax on $100,000 Periodic Registered Plan Withdrawals Comparison

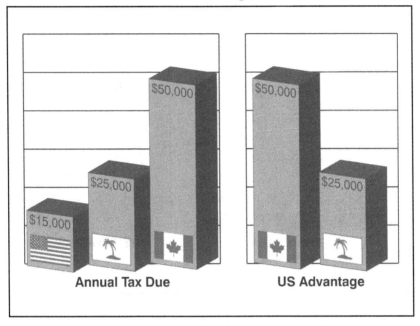

create such tremendous tax savings to those using the US as a tax haven, I have dedicated a large portion of Chapter 8 to discussing RRSPs in more detail.

For Tim and Tara, in this example, a $100,000 withdrawal from an RRSP would attract $50,000 of income tax as Canadian residents. As residents of either the traditional tax haven or the US, the CRA would withhold 25 percent or $25,000 on a $100,000 lump-sum RRSP withdrawal. Therefore, there is no US tax-haven advantage over the traditional tax haven unless Tim and Tara have created a high-tax basis on their RRSP assets before they became US residents, which means close to the entire $25,000 withheld could be recovered. The net result would mean the US would have $50,000 in tax savings over Tim and Tara being Canadian residents, and a $25,000 advantage over the traditional tax haven. See Sample 11.

Tax on $100,000 Lump-Sum RRSP Income Comparison

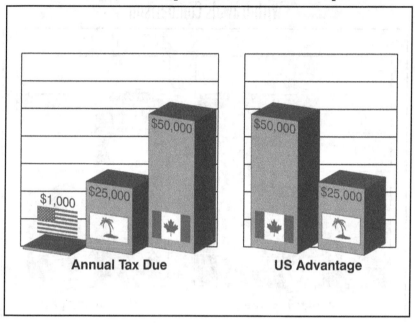

Annual Tax Due   **US Advantage**

9. Canada Pension Plan (CPP) and Quebec Pension Plan (QPP)

Since it is impossible for Tim and Tara to receive $100,000 of the Canada Pension Plan (CPP) or Quebec Pension Plan (QPP) in any given year, we will assume that they each get the annual maximum CPP or QPP of around $10,000 or $20,000 between the two of them. The tax they would pay on $20,000 of CPP or QPP would be $10,000. If they were residents of the traditional tax haven, the tax would drop to $5,000; 25 percent nonresident withholding tax. If they were using the US as a tax haven, the maximum tax rate would be $5,000 or zero dollars if they did the planning and had usable foreign tax credits to reduce their US taxes on this income to zero.

The advantage again goes to the US as the best tax haven for Tim and Tara, with a savings of up to $10,000 over their regular Canadian tax due and $5,000 over a traditional tax haven providing surplus foreign tax credits are available. (If no surplus foreign tax credits are available on the US tax filing for Tim and Tara, the tax paid on CPP or QPP

Tax on $20,000 Canada Pension Plan (CPP) and Quebec Pension Plan (QPP) Income Comparison

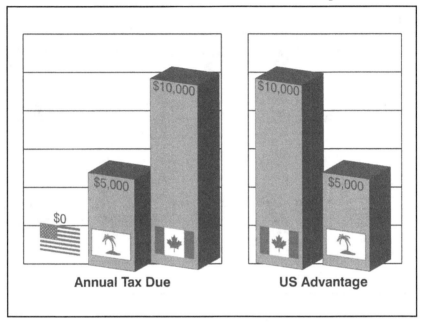

would be roughly equal between the US and the traditional tax haven.) See Sample 12.

10. Old Age Security (OAS)

Under ideal circumstances, the maximum Canadian Old Age Security (OAS) that Tim and Tara could collect would be about $6,000 each for a total of $12,000 for both. However, since they are in the top Canadian income tax brackets, they are subject to the 100 percent OAS claw-back tax, which means that their income tax on the OAS is equal to the OAS pension itself and they get nothing.

Since it takes 40 years as a Canadian resident to qualify for OAS, having it subject to a 100 percent tax because a person was successful is problematic for most Canadians who remain residents of Canada. If Tim and Tara move to the traditional tax haven island, their tax rate on the OAS would remain at the 100 percent total claw-back tax and they would receive nothing from it.

Tax on $12,000 Old Age Security (OAS) Income Comparison

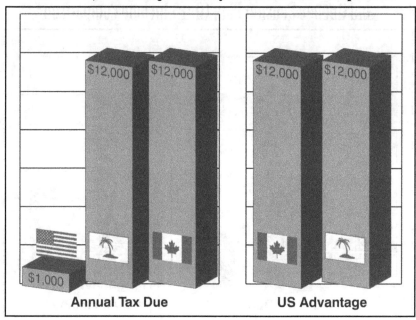

$12,000 $12,000 $12,000 $12,000

$1,000

Annual Tax Due   **US Advantage**

If they move to the US, they get the entire OAS amount and they get a favorable tax rate on it. On the $12,000 of OAS that they would receive in the US, the maximum US tax they would pay would be $3,000 but if they had surplus foreign tax credits, they would pay zero dollars in tax. See Sample 13.

I always joke with Canadians who move to the US and are able to collect the OAS that they would get none of if they still lived in Canada. I tell them to use the funds to take a wonderful cruise every year and send a thank-you note to the Prime Minister!

In summary, for OAS the advantage is far superior when you use the US as your tax haven. For Tim and Tara, the potential tax savings on this income is $12,000 per year over both the traditional tax haven and the Canadian resident tax rates on OAS. Tim and Tara's medical costs in the US would probably be equal to around $500 a month each or $1000 a month total, coincidentally that is approximately equal to what tax they would save on the Old Age Security when moving to the US. Therefore another way to look at this is the Canadian government is actually paying for their US health insurance how sweet is that?

11. Canadian Rental Income

If Tim and Tara had $100,000 of Canadian net (after deducting all expenses and depreciation) rental income from investment properties they held in Canada, their tax in Canada would be the full $50,000. If they moved to a traditional tax haven, they would pay a Canadian nonresident withholding tax of 50 percent or $50,000. If they were using the US as a tax haven, the maximum Canadian tax would drop to the nonresident withholding tax of 25 percent or $25,000.

Since we are assuming they would be in a 30 percent tax bracket in the US, their total tax bill would be $30,000 less the $25,000 credit for the taxes paid to Canada or a net of $5,000. This $5,000 could be covered with a surplus of foreign tax credits so that their net tax would be only the 25 percent withholding paid to the CRA. Advantage for the US tax haven is $25,000 over the traditional tax haven and also $25,000 over the regular tax Tim and Tara would pay as Canadian residents.

The CRA provides provisions that nonresidents may elect to file full Canadian tax returns on rental income rather than be subject to the flat nonresident withholding tax so therefore those going to the traditional tax haven would normally get a slight reduction in tax if they filed Canadian nonresident returns. Because the US tax rates are lower on the net rental income, it would likely be a waste of time and money to file the Canadian nonresident return for those using the US as a tax haven when there is significant net rental income. For those persons moving to the US, they need to calculate whether the 25 percent treaty rate on rental withholding is less than filing a Canadian nonresident return on a net rental income. See Sample 14.

12. Employment Income

For the purposes of this example, employment income includes any salaries, director's fees, consulting fees, or taxable employee benefits that Tim and Tara would earn. However, since being a director of a Canadian company would likely be considered a residential tie, if Tim and Tara moved to the traditional tax haven, they would not likely have the flexibility or opportunity to earn this kind of income. The tax they would pay on the employment earnings in a traditional tax haven would probably be moot.

For the purposes of this illustration we will make the assumption that Tim and Tara earned this income as directors of Canadian companies

Tax on $100,000 Canadian Rental Income Comparison

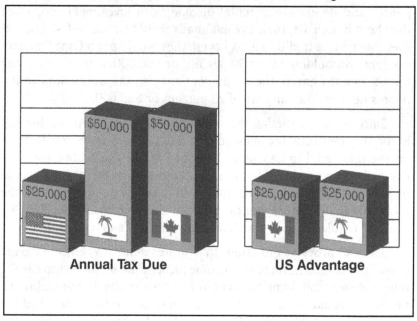

which required them to be in Canada for the directors' meetings. The Canadian tax they would pay on this income would be the ordinary Canadian rates of $50,000 on the $100,000. As a resident of a traditional tax haven, the tax on this income would be identical to the normal Canadian rate as they must file Canadian nonresident tax returns and pay regular Canadian taxes.

If Tim and Tara were using the US as their tax haven, the US tax rate on this income would be 30 percent or $30,000. Since they would be paying $50,000 Canadian, they would get a full credit for what they paid to the CRA which would give them a $20,000 foreign tax credit surplus to possibly use to offset US taxes on other forms of income in the same category. Once more, the advantage goes to the US with $20,000 in savings over the traditional tax haven and the regular Canadian resident tax rates. See Sample 15.

13. Royalties

This example uses the most common kind of royalties, which is royalties produced through Canadian oil and gas properties.

Sample 15
Tax on $100,000 Canadian Employment Income Comparison

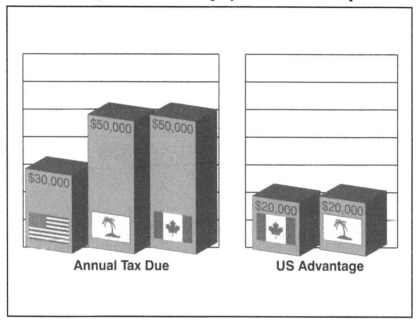

If Tim and Tara earned $100,000 in royalties as Canadian residents, the tax would be the maximum of $50,000. As residents of the traditional tax haven, the tax paid would be a 25 percent (i.e., $25,000) nonresident withholding tax to the CRA.

As US residents, Tim and Tara would pay only 10 percent (i.e., $10,000) nonresident withholding tax to Canada. The royalty would be fully taxable in the US so their total US tax bill would be $30,000 less the $10,000 of foreign tax credits from Canadian withholding, leaving a net US income tax of $20,000. However, as in previous examples, total US taxes due could be paid from surplus foreign tax credits from other sources leaving them at the net (after foreign tax credit out-of-pocket tax) of just the $10,000 treaty withholding tax paid to the CRA.

Once again, with proper foreign tax credit management, the US is a better tax haven than the traditional tax haven with $15,000 less taxes paid on this income. Tim and Tara would have $40,000 less tax to shell out than they would have paid in Canada, without any surplus foreign tax credits. Without surplus tax credits available the tax advantage would be with the traditional tax haven by $5,000 less total tax

Tax on $100,000 Canadian Royalty Income Comparison

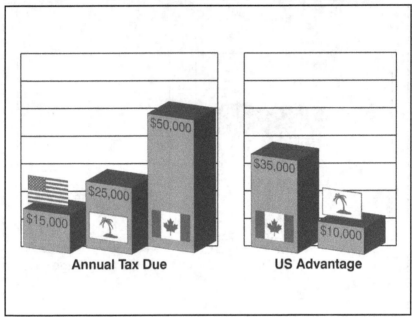

due than the US, and $25,000 less than the tax as Canadian residents. See Sample 16.

14. Who Won the Tax Haven Tax Challenge?

Clearly, Tim and Tara would be big winners as far as tax reductions go by using the US as a tax haven. Because they are in the highest Canadian tax brackets, they would benefit more than those who are not. The key revelation here is, in nearly every single type and source of income, the US is superior to the traditional tax haven for Canadians. This is due primarily to the Canada-US Tax Treaty which, again, is not available to those moving to the traditional tax haven island.

If we total all of the 11 individual types of income at $100,000 each along with CPP or QPP and OAS income in the previous sections, we come up with $1,132,000 from all the various income sources. Although it does not really matter whether Tim and Tara had all this income in one year or over several years, the tax savings result is approximately the same. The US as a tax haven would save them $412,000 in income taxes over what they would have paid as residents of Canada on the same income, and offer a total of $212,000 more as tax reduction (when foreign tax credits are managed most effectively) than the traditional tax haven.

Note: Isolating income types and sources as we have done in the previous sections is fine for illustrative purposes but it is not all that realistic. It is a much more complex matter when filing actual tax returns. There are multiple lines of income, deductions, and credits and the very complex interaction amongst all these items to come up with the bottom line of what tax each taxpayer needs to pay.

There is a good argument in favor of the traditional tax haven with respect to filing tax returns in that, other than nonresident tax returns for Canadian sourced income, there should be little filing requirements since all the tax paid is withheld at the source before it can be distributed. Traditional tax havens do not require an annual tax filing. If there are no surplus foreign tax credits available to use on a US tax return to offset tax on foreign income, the offshore tax haven can win this comparison with the US in a few more of the income types noted, but the overall advantage will remain with the current US tax rates.

Good, comprehensive, forward-looking cross-border plans created by experienced professionals, before moving to either the US or a traditional tax haven, are mandatory for optimal results.

15. Real Results from Real People

The following real examples of tax comparisons clearly display the advantage for Canadians using the US as their tax haven. These numbers come from typical US tax returns prepared by KeatsConnelly and give more accurate and much more realistic results as to whether the US is a better tax haven than the traditional tax haven island as far as income-tax reduction goes. Note that because of the complexity of each individual's situation, results can vary substantially.

I have tried to show you a range of situations and different levels and sources of income so you can get a better idea of where you might fit into the tax results when using the US as a tax haven. Although these examples are typical, the information is changed or disguised so each sample cannot be recognized by anyone and any numbers or circumstances that are the same as a real individual taxpayer situation are strictly coincidental.

To most tax advisors, the proof that the US is an equal or a better tax haven than the traditional tax haven countries comes from actual tax results and comparisons.

We, at KeatsConnelly, have Canadian Chartered Accountants new Canadian professional designation Chartered Personal Accountants (CPA), US Certified Public Accountants (CPAs), US and Canadian Certified Financial Planners) (CFPs) and other tax professionals who over the years have prepared thousands of US and Canadian tax returns for Canadians and Americans living both inside and outside of their respective native countries. Over the years of reviewing all of these complex returns, I found a definite pattern of substantial tax savings for Canadians completing a cross-border move to the US. In short, the results were so spectacular that we started comparing US taxes paid to those paid in traditional tax havens. The surprising bottom line was, in the majority of cases, Canadians actually paid the same or a lower rate of income tax in the US when compared to the traditional tax havens.

In addition, when a broader comparison was done including the "hidden tax" of the tax haven which I discussed in Chapters 2 and 3, the US, for these Canadians, was consistently the hands-down winner for a better lifestyle and lower taxes.

These typical results are from KeatsConnelly filing joint IRS Form 1040 for Canadians that successfully made the transition to the US and were no longer considered Canadian tax-paying residents under the Treaty tiebreaker rules (see Chapter 5). For the particular year filed, the Canadian T1 returns and the withholding for the traditional tax haven are based on the best estimate of the actual tax that would have been paid in Canada or withheld if one were resident of a traditional tax haven without any tax treaty with Canada. Generally, no Canadian returns were actually filed for these individual examples because they were not necessary.

There are numerous examples I could use to illustrate that the proof is in the numbers but I have tried to choose what I would consider more typical situations and persons who were US residents long enough to see the benefits of their lifestyle choices and tax savings. The majority of the couples in these examples have enough income and assets such that Canadian advisors would have possibly recommended these families go to offshore tax havens, with the US likely never even mentioned as an option or eliminated because of the myths perpetuated with the Canadian advisors as discussed in more detail in Chapter 7.

15.1 High-level corporate executive

The first example is a retiring key executive at one of Canada's largest corporations at the time his cross-border plan was developed. His key advisors at the time, in the mid-'90s, were with one of the big four accounting firms provided for and paid for by his company. When he came to KeatsConnelly, after attending one of our Cross-Border Living Workshops, he was looking for better tax-reducing retirement options than what his advisors from the accounting firm were providing. The advice from the big-four accounting firm was, and consisted primarily of "pay the tax in Canada or go offshore." Neither of these options was acceptable to the client because of the client's desired family and lifestyle choices.

This executive had a superior pension and supplementary executive retirement plan provided by his company, as well as real estate in Canada and the US. He and his wife had a combined net worth of more than $10 million including the present value of all pension benefits. Their combined income, which consisted primarily of portfolio income and pension, in the typical tax year after they became US residents in a Sun Belt state with no state income tax for individuals, was around $750,000.

During the dozen or more years after becoming US residents they typically paid a combined husband and wife US tax of less than $10,000 and used foreign tax credits of $60,000, for a total US federal and state tax due of $70,000. The estimated Ontario tax for a typical year was $335,000 if they had remained Canadian residents with the identical income. The estimated tax haven tax for that year would have been in excess of $150,000 consisting primarily of the 25 percent nonresident withholding tax that the CRA would take on his pensions. This tax differential between Canada, the tax haven, and the US had been consistent throughout the approximately 20 years this couple had been US residents. It doesn't take a math major to calculate that this couple saved several millions of dollars in taxes as US residents in retirement rather than going offshore to a typical tax haven, not to mention even larger tax savings when compared with retirement in Canada.

This couple has had a much better lifestyle in the US Sun Belt compared to the tax haven island. On one of those tax haven islands in the middle of nowhere they never would have been able to be close to their family (i.e., children and grandchildren) and receive the kind of medical treatment they have needed over the years.

There is an interesting tax anecdote for this couple. The Canada-US Tax Treaty eliminates the 100 percent Old Age Security (OAS) claw-back tax (a benefit they would not get if they lived in a traditional tax haven or Canada). The savings on their OAS alone amounted to more than $200,000 for the period of residence in the US to date, just for this one simple gift from the CRA through the treaty.

Since this couple invested their OAS clawback savings in their US portfolio, over the approximate 20 years of US residency, their portfolio has grown by at least this additional amount of dollars and provided extra income solely due to the OAS benefits. Although they received these OAS benefits as US residents, they would have had 100 percent clawed back by the CRA either as Canadian residents or residents of a traditional tax haven.

The supplemental executive pension has now been totally paid out, and because of corporate financial difficulties this executive's pension has been reduced, but because of all the tax savings accumulated and invested, portfolio income has replaced the majority of the couple's income needs. Had they remained in Canada or gone offshore the additional tax paid would not be available for them to use today. Because of their former company's bankruptcy and pension reductions they would have been in a very tight financial situation for the rest of their lives without all the tax savings they pocketed by using the US as their tax haven.

15.2 Business owner and entrepreneur

The second example illustrating the US as an equal or better tax haven for Canadians, is a very different set of circumstances consisting of a successful businessman involved in creating, developing, and selling his own companies in the public market. He decided he wanted to retire in the late 1990s and because his adult children and grandchildren were spread throughout the US and Canada, his wife would not agree to go offshore to a traditional tax haven island.

The combined net worth of this couple was in excess of $10 million. In the specific year of calculation, their combined income was $520,000 consisting primarily of investment portfolio income. They paid US federal and state taxes of $33,800 and used foreign tax credits of approximately $60,000 for a total US tax of $93,800. Their estimated Ontario tax for that year was $234,000 and the approximate tax-haven comparative tax was $78,000 plus an additional $12,000 for the OAS claw back for a total of $90,000.

This couple still keeps a large Canadian residence in which they spend four to five months a year with their family and then the remaining seven to eight months they spend at their beautiful US Sun Belt residence close to their children and grandchildren.

Because of their residual business connections, they were able to develop qualifications necessary for free Part A US Medicare, giving them complete access, for the rest of their lives, to the US medical system. This excellent Medicare supplemental insurance coverage is something they never would've been able to achieve had they lived in a traditional tax haven.

This couple specifically requested the option to be able to move back to Canada at some point in the future for family reasons. Since they are protected under the Canada-US Tax Treaty, and they adhere to the CRA and Treaty rules, they will have no problem moving back to Canada if and when they choose to do so. If they had gone to the traditional tax haven, this lifestyle option would be substantially more difficult to achieve without that Treaty protection.

This couple also had a successful Initial Public Offering (IPO) of one of their Canadian companies after they were residents of the US. Because they used the US as their tax haven and with treaty benefits, this IPO, when liquidated for several millions of dollars was tax-free to them, a costly near impossibility had they used the traditional tax haven.

15.3 Broker

This example is about a Canadian broker from a large Canadian brokerage firm who wanted to change careers and move to the US. The broker and his wife had two children living at home and one child married and living in the US. Because this was a change in career and there were still dependent children that need to be educated, an offshore island would have severely stifled this family's opportunity, another limitation to individual lifestyles in offshore jurisdictions.

In the year of calculation, they had income of $1,001,000. They paid US tax of $26,600 and used foreign tax credits of $283,300 for a total US federal and state income tax of $309,900. Their estimated Canadian federal and provincial tax on the same income would have been $380,000 while the tax haven tax would have been around $350,000. The tax haven tax in this instance is difficult to determine for sure because we assisted this broker in negotiating his buyout package from the brokerage firm, such that the majority of the buyout was considered a retirement benefit under the Canada-US Tax Treaty. Absent the treaty, the CRA may have taxed this benefit as full employment income at maximum Canadian rates rather than as a retirement benefit subject to a lower rate of nonresident withholding tax.

15.4 Business owner selling a successful business

This example is that of a typical successful business owner who had worked hard to build a business from nothing to a marketable value in excess of $10 million. His plight was that he had a buyer for his business who only wanted to buy the business assets, which meant he would pay more than 40 percent tax on the sale to the CRA. Using the Canada-US Tax Treaty, the cross-border plan designed by KeatsConnelly in conjunction with a move to the US as a tax haven reduced this tax to just 15 percent. The 15 percent has since been recovered through foreign tax credits in the US and this business owner was able to sell his multimillion-dollar business for a net effective tax rate of zero. Because of this tax rate of zero on the sale, this business owner had one-time tax savings on the sale of his business in excess of $4 million.

After this client was clearly established as a US resident, the comparison year used for this example showed a total income of approximately $480,000. The business owner and his wife paid US taxes of approximately $15,000, and used up foreign tax credits of approximately $75,000. The combined out-of-pocket tax cost for this client for this year was the total of the US tax and the foreign tax credits of $90,000. Had they still been residents of Canada in that same tax year, they would have had to pay Canadian taxes in excess of $300,000. If they were resident in the traditional tax haven, the tax that same year would have been in the neighborhood of $152,000.

15.5 Simply retired

This example is a very basic one with a medical twist. He was a widower in his mid-70s and he married an American widow, in her 60s. They were both of modest income and net worth. They came to KeatsConnelly with the desire to make the right lifestyle and income tax choices where they could enjoy their retirement lifestyle in Canada, the US Sun Belt, or elsewhere.

At the time they came to us they were newly married and had a major medical dilemma. He was on a waiting list for open heart surgery in Canada. Because of his age he was clearly getting the message that he was a low-priority person to the Canadian medical system as he kept getting bumped from his scheduled surgery dates. He was fearful, and rightly so, that he would die while on the Canadian waiting list for surgery. As discussed in Chapter 4, a major lifestyle benefit of using the US as a tax haven is access to the US medical system. We were able to get him on US Medicare and he had surgery done within a couple of months. He's now very healthy and over 90 years old.

This couple's income is approximately $150,000, primarily from their combined private and government pensions. For a typical tax year, their total tax bill consists of about $16,000 withholding on his pensions from Canada and an additional $1,500 tax due to the IRS for a total of around $17,500 annually. Had they made the lifestyle choice to live in Canada, their taxes in Canada would have totaled approximately $70,000 per year including things such as the Old Age Security claw back. If they would have moved to a tax haven island, their tax would have been in the range of $50,000 annually.

As far as both improved lifestyle and substantial tax reduction, the US has been truly a blessing to this couple particularly since he suggests that he is alive and has been able to enjoy his retirement, golfing nearly every day, because he was able to get his heart surgery on US Medicare before he died on the Canadian waiting list for the necessary surgery.

15.6 Teachers

We have helped many clients that are retired teachers and professors. Although their income would not generally be considered high, they usually have a very good pension and ancillary benefits along with lifetime savings from RRSPs and other investments.

The couple in this example has an annual income of $90,000. The Canadian withholding on their pensions is generally around $6,000. There is nothing due to the IRS or to their US state for taxes. In other words, the Treaty-withholding rate on their pensions from Canada totally covers any US taxes that might otherwise be due to the IRS on their pensions and investment income. Had they remained Canadian residents, or if they moved back to Canada, their annual Canadian tax would be in excess of $20,000. If they were residents of a traditional tax haven island their annual tax bill would be in excess of $17,000.

Although the tax benefits received by these retired teachers are not as great in real numbers as some of the other examples in this chapter, it is very significant in improving their lifestyle for their retirement. The extra $15,000 per year in tax savings plus lower cost of living in the US makes this couple's lifestyle work extremely well for them at this point in their lives. We were also able to get them qualified for US Medicare and a Social Security pension.

This is a good example of why Canadians do not need to be in a very high income bracket to benefit from using the US as their tax haven. Because of this couple's income level along with the higher withholding on their pensions, combined with the high cost of living on the traditional tax haven island, living on one of these islands would have been nearly impossible for them to do.

The US Is an Incredible Tax Haven for Small-Business Owners

Being a small-business owner and entrepreneur is no piece of cake. I can identify with the countless hours of trying to climb impossible mountains, putting out fires, handling renegade employees, paying bills, and making payroll. I understand the frustration of dealing with all the government rules and regulations to the extent that sometimes I think I'm actually working for the government! It sometimes feels like the government is making it nearly impossible for business owners to make a profit by conforming to all of its seemingly pointless rules.

I understand the anger and frustration that occurs when a business owner goes to sell all or part of his or her business and the government has its hand out to take a substantial chunk of the business owner's hard-earned equity. This is why it gives me great satisfaction to use cross-border strategies to assist in reducing the tax bite business owners face when selling their business, particularly on the proceeds of the sale after taxes.

No other area of cross-border financial planning offers Canadian owners of small businesses and farms more income tax-saving potential than moving to the United States. A well-thought-out cross-border financial plan can save a business owner or farmer several hundreds of thousands of dollars to several million dollars, depending on the size or the nature of the business.

Most of these planning opportunities arise solely because of the Canada-US Tax Treaty. These tax savings would not be available to business owners if they remained Canadian residents and they were not willing or able to relocate to the US for five years or more. Five years of US residency is not a hard and fast rule; it just gives plenty of time between the date of exit and date of return to Canada if that is what the taxpayer eventually decides to do.

This chapter will outline strategies that are customizable to most business situations. Virtually any kind of business shareholder or farming arrangement amongst family members, partners, or employees can benefit by using the US as their lifestyle choice and tax haven.

1. Uninformed Advisors May Become Obstacles

Unfortunately, a business owner's trusted advisors, accountants, and lawyers sometimes become a major deterrent to making such financial savings happen. Most often these advisors are unaware of the US domestic rules and treaty rules that make it possible to sell a business using treaty planning rather than the normal domestic planning. As a result, the business owner may be inadvertently misled or discouraged from taking advantage of great opportunities such as a much higher net value after taxes on the sale of their business.

Giving a great deal of their lifelong business to Canada Revenue Agency (CRA) is bothersome, to say the least, to the business owner. However, the CRA does get its regular rate of tax or the Treaty rate it is legally able to collect so it does get a piece of the pie, it is just sometimes a smaller slice if the taxpayer leaves Canada to a new tax jurisdiction such as the US. Refer to Chapter 6 to review the 13 primary sources of income where the US has lower tax than the tax paid by Canadian residents.

For the business owner using traditional Canadian domestic tax rules, Canadian advisors may plan to reduce or defer taxes on the sale of the business. This is a tough job at the best of times for typical Canadian advisors to businesses attempting to reduce taxes using CRA domestic rules, so very seldom do these advisors ever consider using the US or the Canada-US Tax Treaty rules to assist their clients in paying less taxes. This is great concern to me because the very people the business owner is relying on are letting them down whether intentionally or not. A simple analogy to this situation is a carpenter using a handsaw and a regular hammer to construct a house when there is a tool shed right next door that has power saws and pneumatic hammers that would get the job done better and faster. The US domestic rules and the Treaty rules available to the business owner are additional tools in the tool shed that should not be ignored by any of the business owner's advisors. The Canadian domestic rules are our tools but they just can't get the job done as well as using all the other tools available in the toolshed. However, as with any tools available from toolshed you need a skilled operator that knows what tool to use and when and how to use it correctly.

Regardless of how the advisors do the planning for the business owner, inevitably the business sale results in a tax rate generally averaging around 30 percent. It depends on the province and whether shares or assets of the business were sold and whether the business qualified for a small-business capital gains exemption. These Canadian advisors will normally set up holding companies to defer some of the average 30 percent tax on the taxable earnings or equity from a business sale. By locking up some of the sale proceeds into Canadian holding companies, often a lower rate of tax on the sale proceeds can be paid with a portion of it deferred until the business owner decides he or she would like to spend the money. Deferred taxes are often okay but there is always a day of reckoning at some point in the future, because tax does need to be paid and often at a higher rate than had it been paid at the time of the sale. The additional income earned in the holding company from the invested proceeds after the sale is taxed at rates higher than the individual taxpayer rates. The Canada Revenue Agency (CRA) and the individual provinces have tried to discourage the use of corporate holding companies to earn investment income by charging this higher rate of tax and in order to normalize the tax to approximately equivalent that the business owner would have paid had they invested the money outside the Corporation they have to dividend the investment earnings out to themselves personally in order that the Corporation gets a refund of a portion of the higher tax paid inside the holding company, this is normally referred to as Refundable Dividend Tax On Hand (RTDOH). I find most business owners are unaware of the fact that they actually pay a higher rate of tax inside their holding companies on investment income until they distribute it out of the Corporation. In any event, deferred taxes on part of the business sell proceeds pale in comparison to good cross-border tax reduction or elimination strategies using a combination of treaty and domestic rules by skillfully using all the tools in the available in the planning toolshed.

2. The Power of Tax Free versus Tax Deferred

If a business owner were to follow the standard Canadian planning using the standard Canadian planning tools laid out by his or her Canadian advisors, to sell a business and either pay all the tax up front or attempt to defer part of it, what does a person do with the remaining net cash after all the Canadian taxes have been paid? The choices here can be critical to enjoying a better lifestyle.

With the funds left over after all the dust has settled and tax paid from the sale of the business or farm, the business owner is now faced with paying ordinary Canadian tax rates on all of the investment income he or she generates from the net proceeds. Consequently, the business owner will pay around 25 percent tax on capital gains, around 35 percent on Canadian dividends, and around 50 percent on interest or US dividends on portfolio income earned outside of a holding company. As noted in the previous section of this chapter investment income inside a typical Canadian holding company actually attracts higher rates than his or her individual portfolio until the income is distributed out of the holding company.

Sample 17 shows a powerful example of the difference between the business owner with proceeds of $10 million after the business has been sold and all Canadian taxes paid (partially deferred or otherwise), and the tax-free investment opportunities available from the US toolshed using the US as a lifestyle choice and tax haven. For ease of illustration in this example, the basic assumption is that the business owner is done with taking risks and, to minimize this risk, invests the entire portfolio in bonds and Guaranteed Investment Certificates (GICs) averaging a total interest rate of 4 percent. The tax rate on this income in Canada would be around 50 percent.

Sample 17 also assumes that the business owner and his or her spouse will live at least 20 years after the sale of their business and they are able to live off of this 4 percent interest after taxes without touching the principal in the $10 million portfolio. In addition, we compare a portfolio of tax-free municipal bonds they could have in the US which would yield them the same 4 percent as to what they would earn on their portfolio in Canada - a reasonable assumption under the current interest rate environment.

Even though Sample 17 seems very simple, it proves several very important points. The first point is that this business owner, over a 20-year period, would have $4 million more to spend after taxes in the

US versus Canada After-Tax Income Comparison

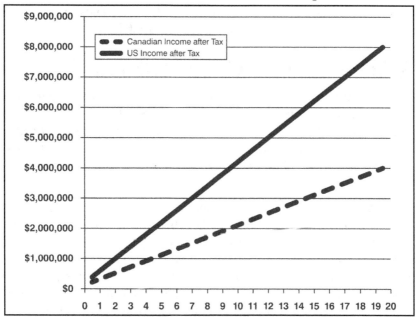

US than in Canada on a similar portfolio with identical return. The second thing this illustrates is that even though the business owner may have paid a lot of taxes on the sale of the business, it may be equally or even more important to understand what to do with the net funds after taxes than it is to try to save taxes on the sale of the business. The third important point is the immense opportunity business owners or farmers, with their hard-earned equity built up over the years, can use in the US to fulfill their desired lifestyle with much more to spend to enjoy that chosen lifestyle while at the same time leaving a much larger legacy to their family.

3. Two Common Myths

If an informed business owner asks long-time Canadian advisors, accountants, or lawyers about moving to the US to help reduce taxes from the sale of a business, he or she is confronted by two or more common myths. The first myth is that you cannot leave Canada because you are going to pay too much exit tax. The second myth is that an estate is too large to move to the US because you will be subject to US estate taxes. Because so many Canadian advisors perpetuate these myths, I feel there are a great number of business owners who have paid substantially more income taxes by following their long-time trusted advisors' advice in this area. (Chapter 9 explains in detail why these and other myths and misconceptions are false.)

4. Larger Capital Gains Exemption Equivalent

Canadian small-business owners are currently limited to a once-in-a-lifetime tax-free capital gains exemption of $800,000, if they meet the CRA requirements to qualify for this exemption on the sale of shares of closely held private businesses. If proper planning has been done, this exemption may be effectively doubled by including a spouse or children as co-owner(s) of the business.

What happens if you have no exemption remaining? Do you need to sell the assets of your company rather than shares? What if your business does not qualify for the exemption or your capital gains exceed the $800,000 exemption limitations? A tax rate, which is currently nearly 25 percent in most provinces, is applied to the amount of capital gains not eligible for the exemption. When assets are sold, often there is a recapture of previous depreciation write-offs that attract an even higher rate of tax (close to 50 percent depending on your province of residence). Often a cross-border planning strategy can be useful when there is no capital gains exemption available because the exemption was used previously or the buyer wanted to buy assets and there were substantial recapture of depreciation and ordinary income tax on the business sale.

How much tax can you save by making the sale using cross-border planning techniques? The short answer is, "It depends." The range of savings can be negligible relative to the Canadian domestic rates noted above or, at best, the total tax rate can be reduced to the Treaty withholding rate of taxes for dividends paid from the Canadian company of 5 or 15 percent. If coordinated with US immigration, the tax paid to the CRA is often times completely recovered in the US through foreign tax credits on income generated by a properly designed investment portfolio or other foreign tax-credit planning methods. Foreign tax credits are a very useful tool available in the planning toolshed that is not available to a business owner if they rely on the limited tools available on the sale of their business when they remain in Canada.

Between the Canada-US Tax Treaty and the IRS's rules concerning foreign tax credits, this tax paid on the sale of the business can normally be fully recovered over ten years. The net result is that a successful business owner can sell his or her business and effectively pay very low taxes, even close to zero net tax, depending on how the use of the foreign tax credits falls in his or her favor. This low net-tax scenario can apply if the proceeds from the business are $500,000, $5 million, $50 million, or more!

These potential tax savings can be obtained based on legal precedents. The key point is that business owners should be aware that significant tax savings are still possible and available. To use a cross-border plan to maximum advantage, business owners and their advisors need to seek the services of a qualified cross-border financial-planning specialist that is able to bring to the table a great deal of additional tools from the cross-border planning toolshed early in the process of retiring or selling their businesses. In fact, if a cross-border planning specialist is brought in early enough, the planning can actually facilitate the retirement process — or transition to family members or third parties — while simultaneously providing major tax advantages to the purchaser and the owner.

4.1 Brother to brother

A good example of such a situation is a case in which two brothers equally owned a multimillion-dollar business in Alberta. The older of the two brothers wanted to retire to his winter home in Arizona, but a study the brothers had commissioned from one of the big four accounting firms in Alberta told them there wasn't enough cash flow from the business for the younger brother to buy out the older one and pay all the taxes due. The accountants and company bankers also told them that if they borrowed the money to complete the sale, the debt load would likely sink the business. For more than two years these brothers sought someone to help them through this dilemma.

The brothers were referred to me by another client, and within a year the older brother was golfing in Arizona, and the younger brother owned the business. Everyone was happy, including CRA, because it got its taxes when the business was sold. The younger brother was able to keep the business and had sufficient cash flow to pay off his older brother. The older brother had substantially reduced taxes because he now lived in the US and the IRS was happy because they had a new taxpayer. Now, well over ten years later, the younger brother has transitioned this very successful business to a third party and his son.

The younger brother was able to save substantially in income taxes for himself and his family by taking up US residency.

5. Operating a Canadian Business from the US

A Canadian business owner living in the US, who continues to own an active Canadian business or holding company, needs to create new entities or reorganize the existing corporation to prevent potential double tax on corporate income.

If the Canadian company is largely a passive one earning income from rentals and investments, it will likely be considered a foreign personal holding company or controlled foreign corporation by the IRS and be subject to many reporting and other requirements. For example, if the company's fiscal year does not end on December 31, calendar-year reporting of the corporate income must be provided, and tax must be paid as if the shareholders personally owned the corporate assets. This tax must be paid whether or not income is actually distributed to the shareholders that year. Considering all of the IRS reporting requirements on foreign holding companies, there is little to no advantage, and there are many disadvantages including higher taxes, to maintaining a Canadian passive investment company of this type.

I would normally recommend the company be unwound before or shortly after US residence is taken, or that it be converted to a BC, Nova Scotia, or Alberta Unlimited Liability Company. The Unlimited Liability Company is taxed like a partnership for US purposes, so all income flows through to the owner, to be taxed only once in the US with full foreign tax credits for taxes paid in Canada by the corporation.

Canadian companies owned by US residents or citizens reporting active business income are also subject to special rules on reporting income. The earnings and profits from an active Canadian company that are retained in the company will not flow through to the US shareholder on an accrual basis, and generally, the tax to this shareholder may be deferred until the earnings and profits are withdrawn. However, deferring tax on the accrued income in the corporation does not eliminate the double-tax problem on this income unless the corporation is converted to an unlimited liability company. In order to maintain the small business tax rate on the first $500,000 of earnings business owner moving to the US would have to recapitalize the Corporation to ensure that at least 50 percent of the voting control remained in Canada. The voting control could be transferred to children or a Canadian trust that would remain resident in Canada.

With an active Canadian company, and to a lesser extent a holding company, one very good method to reduce corporate income from the operation is to collect a reasonable management fee, which could zero out the corporate net income. The Canadian corporation would be able to deduct the management fee in full. Under the Canada-US Tax Treaty, management fees are subject only to a maximum 15 percent withholding tax. The 15 percent withholding tax is fully recoverable in the US through the foreign tax credits allowed by the IRS.

If the actual management work is done on the US side of the border, the Canadian company can pay a reasonable management fee to the owner, or to a related US company exempt from Canadian withholding. Care must be taken when paying these kinds of fees on a cross-border basis in order not to violate the CRA's transfer pricing rules. The net result is that income can be removed from the Canadian company without Canadian tax and taxed at the lower US rates. The final tax rate paid will be determined by the owner's marginal tax rate and his or her state of residence. If Canadian salaries are taken by US resident shareholders for services provided while in Canada, the shareholders would have to file nonresident Canadian returns and pay tax on the Canadian salary. The Canada-US Tax Treaty states that if the salary is less than $10,000 annually, a Canadian return does not need to be filed and no Canadian tax paid.

6. Tax-Free Rollovers on Investment Real Estate

One of the greatest deterrents for Canadians owning or wishing to invest in US real estate either as their living, their sole business, or as a pure investment strategy to supplement their investment portfolio is the tax when the time comes to sell. In Canada, a sale of the property with capital gains tax and recapture taxes, depending on the province, can take from just under a quarter to just under half of their gains. Not only does this create cash-flow problems for the investors, but if they wish to reinvest the net proceeds into a new project or some other investment, they have substantially less cash available for new investments.

The US can be an excellent tax haven for Canadians wishing to take advantage of real estate investments because of the IRS section 1031 exchange program, another great tool available from the US toolshed. The 1031 exchange allows any real estate investor to take all of the gains from one real estate investment (or other business property) and roll the gain without tax into a new or series of real estate projects, that need to be identified within a reasonable period of time after the sale of the current property. In short, this means real estate investors have use of their money that would otherwise have gone into taxes to purchase more investment real estate. This allows them to make even further gains on money they would have never had available for their own use if they lived in Canada. These US 1031 exchange gains can be deferred for an entire lifetime and then at death the IRS allows a tax holiday by giving a step-up on the cost basis on all of the property gains so any beneficiaries can sell all of the property owned by the deceased without capital gains tax. Any real estate investors can easily realize how much money they can make on the money that would normally go to the tax man; over a lifetime this can be an incredible amount of savings.

Even though real estate investors living in traditional tax havens have no income tax to pay in the country of residence, they always have to pay tax to the country in which the real estate is located. Canadians living in the US who wish to invest in real estate and use the 1031 exchange program to its fullest (although the 1031 exchange is available to nonresident investors, it is very difficult for them to get the same advantage as a US resident), can get substantially better tax results on their US real estate investments than persons living in Canada or outside of the US on one of the island tax havens. Zero percentage income tax on a lifetime of US real estate gains, which could be in the millions of dollars, is very difficult for any Canadian to achieve when comparing the US to the traditional tax-haven countries since this planning tool is not available in the Canadian toolshed.

7. The Unreal-Real Billionaire

Income taxes have been in the news a lot in the US over the past few years, with the expiration and then extension of the so-called Bush tax cuts of 2001. This public debate on taxes between the US Republican and Democratic elected politicians will continue at least through to 2016 and likely well beyond. In the middle of this public debate, Warren Buffett stepped up to the plate and made his tax records partially public.

Mr. Buffett's annual adjusted gross income for 2010 was approximately $63 million. The US adjusted gross income is total income after certain allowed adjustments but before all the deductions have been taken. Mr. Buffett paid personal income taxes of $6.9 million, which is an 11 percent average tax rate.

Although Warren Buffett is not a Canadian seeking to use the US as a tax haven, he certainly is exploiting the best of the US tax system to keep himself in a low tax rate on a spectacular income. How does he do this? He simply takes the majority of his income in the form of dividends, tax-free municipal bond interest, and capital gains. Both dividends and capital gains are taxed at a maximum rate of 20 percent and there is no tax on the municipal bond interest. This is the same choice that most US business owners can take, including Canadian business owners using the US as their tax haven. For some Canadian business owners doing the planning described in this book, they can have tax rates below Warren Buffett's, particularly when they have a surplus of foreign tax credits generated from planning prior to leaving Canada. It should be noted as of January 1, 2013, Mr. Buffett is now subject to the 3.8 percent ObamaCare tax on his dividends and capital gains as noted in Chapter 6, so therefore his average tax rate is probably now just over 20 percent. This is still very reasonable based on such an incredibly high income.

There is one item that needs to be pointed out with respect to Warren Buffett's low tax rate on the dividend portion of his income. Dividends, in order to be paid from one of his corporations, require that the corporation has paid tax on the income before distribution. Consequently, his corporations could have paid as much as 35 percent tax on this income before it was distributed to him as a dividend. This is the classic business/personal double tax and, in Canada, the primary reason why there are dividend tax credits; to adjust for the taxes the corporation has already paid on the income.

Most US small-business owners use flow-through corporations that have no corporate level of tax, so there is only one level of tax at the personal rates. These US flow-through corporations avoid any potential double tax on business income.

The Greatest Opportunities: Retirement Savings Plans

Through my long and varied experience in assisting Canadians and Americans alike with their cross-border lifestyle and financial planning wishes, two critical things rise to the top, as both the greatest area of potential tax savings and at the same time the greatest need. The first of these two areas was comprehensively discussed in Chapter 7. For business owners and farmers there is a great need combined with a great potential for tax reduction using US cross-border planning strategies made available through the application of superior tools available in the US domestic and Treaty toolshed. Chapter 7 discussed many of the opportunities for business owners and farmers but many people don't have a business or a farm, yet still have the need for a change in lifestyle and a tax reduction.

Opportunities are great for Canadians who have one or more of the following plans:

- Registered Retirement Savings Plan (RRSP).
- Registered Retirement Income Fund (RRIF).
- Locked-In Retirement Account (LIRA).
- Life Income Fund (LIF).
- Retirement Compensation Arrangement (RCA).

- Deferred Profit-Sharing Plan (DPSP).

- Individual Pension Plan (IPP).

Canadians are traditionally very good savers and one of the best places they like to save is in registered plans. Many Canadians use RRSPs because they are tax deductible, and they are one of the few tax-saving programs through which Canadians can invest. Routine RRSP deposits and compounding returns are more often than not a Canadian's largest liquid asset in his or her later years so they are worth reviewing in this chapter.

Many Canadians have small fortunes sitting in their RRSPs but are reluctant to withdraw any money from them because they face such high rates of taxation on the withdrawals. Even though this section continually refers to RRSPs, consider them a proxy for the other Canadian registered plans noted in the list. The income tax a person faces on these registered plans is very similar regardless of the type of registered plan for lump-sum withdrawals. Periodic withdrawals, as defined by the CRA, are taxed much more favorably in the United States than on a traditional tax haven island (see Chapter 6, section 8.).

All Canadian registered plans generate similar foreign tax credits and similar planning opportunities for US residents. This chapter will deal with some of the cross-border financial planning tools and techniques that can help you withdraw very large sums from your RRSP and effectively pay a greatly reduced tax. Sometimes, with the right circumstances and planning, you don't pay net taxes at all after recovery of all of the foreign tax credits in the US.

1. Nearly All Registered Plans Are Taxed Identically

Chapter 6 discussed both general and specific circumstances in which an individual using the US as a tax haven beats the traditional tax haven in the amount of tax reduction available to Canadians, both for lump-sum withdrawals and periodic RRSP withdrawals. Regardless of which non-Canadian country in which you are resident, when you make lump-sum withdrawals the CRA always gets the 25 percent nonresident withholding tax.

However, if the US is your tax haven choice, the treaty reduces the tax on periodic RRSP withdrawals to only 15 percent, about a 70 percent reduction over the standard Canadian tax in most provinces on the same withdrawal. It is administratively difficult to make periodic withdrawals from an RRSP. It is easier to convert the RRSP to an RRIF.

The conversion of an RRSP to an RRIF may be completed at any time prior to age 72, when it becomes mandatory under CRA rules. Periodic withdrawals from the RRIF of up to 10 percent, or two times the annual CRA required minimum withdrawal based on age, whichever is greater, is at the 15 percent treaty rate for US residents. Those persons resident in the traditional tax haven island are always stuck with the 25 percent withholding tax on their RRSP-type income rather than periodic or lump-sum.

The issue of what to do with RRSPs when Canadians leave Canada to take up residency in the US or elsewhere is often overlooked, especially for those who fail to complete a cross-border financial planning analysis prior to leaving Canada. When taking up residency in the US, Canadians can find their RRSPs a great source of tax savings if they plan for them correctly.

Without proper planning RRSPs can create unnecessary US taxes and can potentially be double taxed or overtaxed by the US and Canada. Most people ignore planning for their RRSPs thinking there is nothing they need to do. Often they have even been specifically, but quite erroneously, advised to leave their RRSPs in Canada by unknowledgeable or self-serving advisors wishing to earn commissions and fees. Generally, many Canadians let their RRSPs sit and accumulate interest and other investment income innocently, as if they were still residents of Canada.

2. What Does the IRS Think of RRSPs?

How Canadian RRSPs are viewed by the IRS will help explain some of the problems surrounding them and illustrate how you can take advantage of the differences in the rules to save taxes if you are going to use the US as your tax haven. Once you become a US taxpayer, the IRS considers your RRSP an ordinary investment by looking right through the RRSP trusteeship and the CRA's deferment of income tax rules.

The IRS deems an RRSP to be a simple grantor trust, under US rules, on which the grantor (i.e. you, the contributor) pays tax on all the income as it is earned or realized inside the plan. Consequently, the IRS considers an RRSP the same way it would treat the underlying investments of the RRSP just as if the RRSP had not been a registered investment. For example, if you, as a US resident, earned bank interest accruing inside your RRSP located in Canada, the IRS would want you to report and pay tax on that interest as if you had earned it on your regular bank account.

The IRS considers the contributions you made to the RRSP before you became a US resident, as well as the cumulative interest, realized gains, or dividends in it as tax paid principal under the grantor trust rules. (Note that the IRS tax-paid treatment for interest and dividends does not apply to unrealized capital gains unless they are realized prior to you becoming a taxpayer in the US. It doesn't apply to US citizens or green card holders who have been resident in Canada.) Once you are a US resident, citizen, or green card holder, the IRS will tax the interest earned and paid inside the RRSP. Similarly, dividends and capital gains in an RRSP account are subject to US tax as they are paid or realized each and every year, without the deferral of tax provided by the CRA. At first glance this seems like a major problem, but knowing how the IRS taxes RRSPs and similar plans gives cross-border financial planning practitioners a great tool to help Canadians get their RRSPs out of Canada at low or possibly no net taxes.

2.1 RRSP phantom income

If you were to make a mistake and leave your RRSPs in Canada, regardless of where you live in the US, the IRS will tax you as a US resident on all the interest, dividends, and capital gains earned on your account, even though you may not have actually received these funds. This income that you are taxed on but you don't actually receive is called "phantom income."

Many Canadians with RRSPs who have been in the US for years never realized they have US tax liability on the phantom income. The Canada-US Tax Treaty protocol that came into effect in 1996 allows you to make an election annually on your US return to defer the payment of US tax on the RRSP phantom income until such time as it is actually withdrawn. In September 2014 IRS introduced new rules for Canadians living in the US that have Canadian RRSPs to provide them a default election to defer payment of US tax on the earnings inside the RRSP automatically without needing to file a specific election that had been previously required using IRS Form 8891.

Note that if you live in a state that has state income tax, the state income tax may also be due on the phantom income every year, regardless of whether you filed the election with your federal tax return. (Individual US states that do not have a state income tax are not party to the treaty or its elections although some states, such as Arizona, do honor the treaty deferral at the federal level voluntarily.)

In my other book, *The Border Guide*, I spend a fair bit more time explaining the technicalities of RRSPs for US residents and citizens and I outline the top ten reasons you shouldn't leave RRSPs or similar registered investments in Canada once you become a US resident. The long and the short of it is, you simplify your life and get the best tax results if you plan staged withdrawals even before you leave Canada, so that you can spread the withdrawals over one or more years once you become a US resident and can maximize the use of foreign tax credits created by the RRSPs.

There are no provisions between Canada and the US for direct transfer of your RRSP or other registered investment to the US equivalent, an Individual Retirement Account (IRA). You have only three options:

- Withdraw the RRSPs.

- Report the realized income each year and pay the tax on the phantom income.

- Use the annual automatic deferment of tax on the income under the Treaty and the new IRS rules.

If you are intending to reside permanently or at least for five or more years in the US, the first solution — withdrawal of the RRSPs relatively soon after becoming a US resident — is by far the best alternative.

3. Locked-In Retirement Accounts

Canadians who have worked for employers with pension plans within Canada find, much to their disappointment, that a good portion of their pension benefit is "locked in" when they leave the company before retirement age. This lock-in is a result of employment pension plan regulation at the provincial level. All provinces and territories with the exception of PEI have such legislation, which is designed to prevent employees from spending their accrued pension benefits before retirement age. If a company's operations are regulated by the federal government, regardless of in which province or territory the company is located, its pension plans are federally regulated or locked in under the federal guidelines that parallel these provincial lock-in rules. In effect, the provinces and the federal government feel employees aren't responsible enough to roll their pension benefits into an RRSP and leave them there for their eventual retirement, so they force employees to roll the vested company contributions of their pensions into a Locked-In

Retirement Account (LIRA) or a Life Income Fund (LIF). Funds cannot be withdrawn from a LIRA before the plan's normal retirement age, except in specific emergency situations as defined by the applicable provincial or federal legislation.

The normal retirement age is set by the original company plan in which the employee was a member. The LIRA owners, if they wish to make withdrawals, can convert their LIRAs to LIFs. The LIFs operate similar to RRIFs except that the start date at which withdrawals can be made for most provinces is age 55 and there is a maximum withdrawal rate each year, as well as the usual minimum withdrawal amount.

One additional option for LIRA holders is to use LIRA funds to purchase a life annuity which simply provides the plan owner equal monthly payments from the account for life from an insurance company. This is very much like creating your own pension, and the monthly pension amount is dependent on the amount of funds you have in the LIRA to purchase the annuity, and the interest rate that insurance company pays on the funds adjusted for your age at the time of purchase.

All of these lock-ins and restrictions on LIRAs or LIFs make reporting onerous once a Canadian owning these plans becomes a US resident, which makes planning for the most efficient tax savings much more difficult, if not impossible.

After much lobbying of provincial governments to provide relief for nonresident owners of LIRAs, Alberta, British Columbia, Manitoba, Saskatchewan, Ontario, Quebec, and New Brunswick finally came through with legislation that allows LIRA owners from these provinces to break the lock-ins on their LIRAs. All they need is written confirmation from the CRA that they are indeed nonresidents of Canada by completing CRA form NR73. Employees of federally regulated industries such as airlines, railroads, and communication companies, regardless of the province or territory of residence, can also qualify to break the lock-ins on their LIRAs obtained while working with these companies. Most of the provinces and the federal government require that you be a nonresident of Canada for at least two years before you will be allowed to break the lock-in on LIRAs. Alberta and New Brunswick have no two-year waiting period to break the lock ins and as mentioned earlier PEI has no locked-in plans at all that we need to deal with.

Now that seven provinces and the federally regulated companies allow the lock-in to be broken when these LIRA owners become nonresidents of Canada, they can get the same benefits as regular RRSP and RRIF owners along with the resulting tax savings. Being able to break the lock-in on RRSPs by using the US as a tax haven adds to their lifestyle because of the flexibility of being free from the lock-in rules they would have been subject to for the rest of their lives in Canada, the obvious tax savings, and the potential for increased retirement after-tax income. This is indeed another powerful tool available in the cross-border planning toolbox for Canadians looking at using the US as a tax haven that is just not in the Canadian resident toolbox at all.

4. Hire a Professional Cross-Border Financial Planner

Even though getting the best US tax haven results from Canadian registered plans may seem simple, there is a fair bit of complexity. An optimized solution is to remove your RRSP or other registered plan out of Canada with as close to zero net tax as possible. This is one of the clear US tax-haven strategies that no one should attempt to implement on their own. As emphasized back in chapter 7, it is one thing to have these cross-border planning tools available for major tax reduction with RRSPs and LIRAs available but it is another thing to have somebody that knows how to use the tools correctly in a timely fashion. There are too many "forks in the road" that can take you in the wrong direction and can either increase your tax bill or make you miss incredible opportunities with foreign tax credits.

I recommend you use an experienced cross-border financial planner trained in the use of all the tools in the cross-border planning toolbox and all the aspects of Canadian and US investments and tax. A cross-border financial planner is well worth the cost and he or she can provide a great return/value added on the time and dollars spent. In Chapter 6, for Tim and Tara with the $100,000 of RRSP withdrawals, their income tax savings can range from $22,000 to $50,000 depending on how well the planning is laid out and implemented. This is a huge range, with most Canadians settling for the lower dollar savings without proper planning.

Rather than paying the 15 percent or 25 percent treaty withholding rate on the RRSPs once you are a resident of the US, recovering foreign tax credits from the IRS created through the withholding tax on withdrawal of the funds from Canada may often result in achieving zero net tax. The recovery of foreign tax credits requires a custom-designed investment portfolio or other foreign income generator strategies to generate the types of income that will utilize foreign tax credits efficiently.

It is extremely rare to find anyone in the US who can do these specially managed portfolios to the extent necessary. Certainly, many large investment firms could do the customized investment but they sometimes lack the specific cross-border planning expertise to make it happen. (See Chapter 10 for information about choosing qualified advisors.)

If you take into consideration that many Canadians have RRSP balances in the hundreds of thousands of dollars, or even millions of dollars, planning can pay off big. By expanding on the Tim and Tara example from Chapter 6, Sample 10 or 11, to a $1 million RRSP withdrawal instead of just $100,000, the savings are magnified ten times. A few thousand dollars expended for an experienced cross-border planner could provide up to an additional $250,000 tax savings than without planning — a substantial amount to add to a comfortable lifestyle.

Realizing the Dream

The first step to gaining the desired lifestyle and potential cost of living and tax savings by using the US as your tax haven is a critical one. Your choices will affect the rest of your life either positively or negatively, depending on which path you pursue. I enjoy using factual stories to illustrate complex situations, both financial and non-financial, that life presents to us. I will use a few real anecdotes to assist my readers in understanding what they are facing when they embark on the major lifestyle choice of perhaps spending more time in their favorite tropical destination during the long Canadian winters, or perhaps even moving there lock, stock, and barrel.

This first illustration is a personal, non-financial one. My wife Barbara had an important medical decision to make. After we went through this process, I realized what my wife went through was exactly the same thing other Canadians seeking a lifestyle of warm weather and low taxes are confronted with. All too frequently, these Canadians end up in the wrong tax haven on an island in the middle of nowhere, or perhaps feel locked into Canada due to circumstances created by the very wealth they built up over their lifetime to allow them freedom of choice. They hire professionals to give them direction but often things do not follow the best possible path for the very reasons illustrated in this story. At the end of the story I explain how and why these critical choices as related in this personal story are very relevant to the decisions Canadians face when seeking assistance in obtaining their desired cross-border lifestyle.

After a routine visit to her doctor, Barbara was told that she might need surgery. Her regular doctors stated that she should see a surgical specialist for a confirmation and she was referred to one of those specialists to help make the determination of whether surgery was indeed necessary.

My wife visited the specialist she was referred to in her regular doctor's network and that specialist confirmed that she did need surgery. However, the surgery she needed would require not only this specialist's surgery skills, but would require a second surgeon with a separate, board-certified specialty to do additional surgery and so Barbara was referred to a second specialist. Both surgeries would best be done at the same time so that would mean two separate surgical specialists would have to be coordinated to be there in the operating room for a five-hour surgery, and work together to a successful conclusion for my wife.

After an initial consultation with these surgical specialists, my wife was not comfortable that she was getting the full story with respect to her complete set of options. In addition, it seemed to Barbara more that she was being told what she had to do as opposed to being offered alternatives.

Barbara's level of discomfort with trying to coordinate two surgeons was quite understandable. Not only is it difficult to go through surgery when you have one surgeon, but having two means you more than double your chances of something going wrong. Specialists, medical or otherwise, tend to operate in silos so there is a very big question of whether they can work together for a successful conclusion. Also, if something did go wrong there could be plenty of finger-pointing between the two surgical specialists.

These factors motivated my wife to conduct some more thorough research and lo and behold she found there was at least one specialist (later we found out there were five) in the Phoenix area that had a double board-certified practice. This dually qualified surgeon had completed hundreds of successful surgeries for Barbara's exact medical conditions and he was board certified in both surgical disciplines needed to do my wife's surgery. In addition, because this surgeon was an experienced professional he did very few other types of surgery. Consequently, he was able to do the surgery without implanting any permanent medical devices. The other two individual surgeons, who were not doubly certified, told Barbara implants were necessary.

In spite of the fact this surgeon's office and surgical hospital were a lot farther away than where the two separate individual specialist offices were, my wife felt it was well worth the extra half-hour of driving time each way. This was an extremely comforting situation for my wife since she would not have to go through the anxiety and the extra time and effort to coordinate two surgeons. The probability of a successful outcome from her operation was greatly improved and it would take less than three hours instead of five. If something was to go wrong she had one surgeon to hold responsible and wouldn't get in the middle of a fight between the two others she was referred to by her regular doctor. She also did not have to deal with the thought of having to live with surgical devices implanted in her for the rest of her life.

My wife completed the surgery through this specialized surgeon and her quality of life is pretty well back to normal.

Why is this anecdote of my wife's recent surgery a metaphor for Canadians seeking a tropical cross-border lifestyle and tax relief? Unfortunately, I have seen situations like this play out like a bad movie over and over again for Canadians seeking specialized US and Canadian cross-border financial planning advice.

To get the complete picture, please reread this story for a second time. However, the second time substitute yourself for my wife; your long time accountant or lawyer for the regular doctor; a friend or associate of the accountant or lawyer for the first surgery specialist; and a friend of the first specialist for the second specialist (to be successful with a complex cross-border plan you would need a specialist on the Canadian side and a second from the US or a tax haven island). Finally, substitute a dually certified specialist in Canada and the US for the dually certified surgeon, and instead of surgery substitute your cross-border lifestyle planning, and you will understand exactly why this comparison is so relevant.

In summary, this story illustrates several critical considerations in deciding how to get professional help to enrich your cross-border lifestyle:

- Your long-time accountant/lawyer is most likely going to refer you to someone in his or her own firms or close network rather to the best person for the job.

- Just because you know and trust your long-time accountant or lawyer it is not reasonable to expect him or her to be able to do the job and assist you with the complex multi-disciplinary planning and implementation of a cross-border move. These long-time current advisors, regardless of how well they know how to use the Canadian planning tools in the tool shed, seldom know what tools are available in the cross-border planning tool shed and when they do they hardly ever know how to them it properly.

- The accountants' and lawyers' respective codes of conduct require them to disclose to you their lack of qualification, knowledge, or experience in providing you the advice you seek and need. It is most certainly in your best interest to have qualified people doing complex work you need done and if your own advisor fails to disclose they can't provide you what you need, is that in your best interest or theirs?

- The specialist your accountant/lawyer may refer you to be may not be a dually qualified professional specialist in cross-border planning who can cover all the bases for you absolutely need covered and may have to refer you to a second specialist which someone (likely you) will need to coordinate.

- Two singly qualified specialists are unlikely to refer you to a particular professional who is dually qualified in both specialties needed so that they may earn fees for themselves and protect their turf, not to mention potentially doubling your costs.

- A doubly qualified specialist in cross-border financial planning is going to know shortcuts and many tricks of the trade that singly specialized advisors just don't know or understand. Again the analogy of having someone who knows how to use tools in the tool shed quickly and efficiently.

- If you can find a dually qualified specialist you make your life substantially easier, save money, and are probably going to have a better outcome.

- If something is not completed correctly, having one advisor to hold responsible, although unpleasant, is much easier than getting in the middle of a finger-pointing exercise between two other separately qualified professionals, one possibly in Canada and one in the US.

- Because it takes considerable additional time and cost for a professional to become a dually qualified specialist, whether it is in the medical field or the cross-border financial planning area, very few professionals make the effort. Consequently, finding a dually qualified specialist does take a little bit of extra research and effort and often requires you to bypass or ignore your current accountant/lawyer. However, once located, the dually qualified specialist can actually be a time saver, a considerable cost reducer, and provide improved tax benefits on top of providing you a smoother and more solid transition to your new lifestyle.

In Chapter 10, I describe what kind of dually qualified specialist you need to assist you in finding the best lifestyle and lowest taxes, and where to find one.

1. Overcoming the Myths

Earlier this year I was asked by a client to meet with his long-time trusted accountant. This client had made a substantial multimillion-dollar investment in US real estate. He wanted us to do an analysis of whether or not it would be worth it for him and his wife to move to the US Sun Belt where most of his US property was located. The client wanted me to meet his accountant so that I could get a clear picture of his situation in Canada as the first step in completing a cross-border analysis.

The accountant was a well-qualified senior partner in what would be categorized as a midsize regional accounting firm. Included in the meeting were the accountant and two junior colleagues from the accounting firm, the client, his wife, and myself. The client started by laying out the reason and the agenda for the meeting which was to have the accountant and his firm give me the data I needed to make a complete cross-border analysis for the client to see if they could get more out of their cross-border lifestyle with less taxes.

Rather than doing as the client asked and providing me the information I needed, the accountant laid out three myths as to why this client should not even be having this discussion. The thought that went through my mind was (besides why the accountant is ignoring the client's request), "another accounting professional acting in his own self-interest rather than in the best interest of the client and his wife." It was because the accountant was so experienced and had a successful accounting practice that I was moved to action by this meeting and what he said. He either did not understand the myths he was perpetuating, or he had his own self-interest agenda, or both.

The legal and accounting profession, both in Canada and the US, have codes of ethics that are supposed to guide the professionals to bow out of trying to give clients advice in areas of expertise in which they have no knowledge, training, or credentials. If this accountant were acting in his client's best interest and following the code of ethics, he should have told the client he had no US credentials and, therefore, was not qualified to render adequate advice on moving to the US. However, he certainly could provide me with the information I needed on the client's historical financial data that the accounting firm had gathered over many years of working for the client.

This encounter, along with several similar situations, was primarily the motivation for me to write this book. It reminded me of the scope of the obstacles Canadians face when trying to get the appropriate advice from their long-term advisors when they talk about tax-reduction strategies and lifestyle choices. I feel the Canadian advisors who put their own self-interest ahead of clients' lifestyle choices and desires are reprehensible; they are taking advantage of their long-trusted relationship with clients. Who are they to tell the clients how to live their lives? They should not hinder the clients' chosen lifestyle goals because of their own interests.

In Chapter 7, I touched briefly on two of the three myths this accounting partner dumped on us at the start of this meeting. Here I will explain in more detail why this accountant was clearly off track with the advice he was trying to convince his client of and why he was perpetuating an all-too-common set of myths. I'm still mystified as to how such an experienced Canadian Chartered Accountant would be ignorant of the myths he was perpetuating unless he understood them fully and was trying to run a blocking strategy to prevent his client from moving to the US and not requiring as much of his service as the client once did.

1.1 Substantial exit tax

The first myth this accountant dumped on the boardroom table was to deliberately discourage the client and his wife: "You can't leave the country because you will have a substantial exit tax that you need to pay the Canada Revenue Agency before you leave Canada."

This is a myth for numerous reasons, especially in this client's case since most of his assets were invested in real estate. Canadian real estate or companies holding primarily Canadian real estate are considered taxable Canadian property and under the Canada Revenue Agency

(CRA) rules are not subject to deemed disposition tax upon leaving Canada. The main reason why Canadian real estate is not subject to any exit tax is the fact that the real estate cannot be moved with the client. Therefore, even if the client leaves Canada, the CRA will always have the right to collect tax on rent from this property or tax on capital gains on a sale of the property. If the tax is not paid, as legally required, the CRA may simply seize the property or go after the seller and the buyer's lawyers for not withholding the proper nonresident's tax.

The second reason why this client, or anyone else for that matter, would have no exit tax is, if there was a deemed disposition or exit tax due on any of the client's non-Canadian real estate assets, the client could elect under Canadian rules to defer the tax due until the time he actually sold the asset. What this CRA election does is keep the client in exactly the same tax situation as if he had remained in Canada without exiting and held the appreciated asset for sale at a time he chose. Hence, no exit tax and no interest on the deferment of this tax. A client negotiates with the CRA what collateral he or she needs to provide to assure the CRA that it will be able to collect the tax on the investment with the deferred gain when it is finally sold. There is either no deemed disposition tax on most Canadian assets or there is the ability to elect out of the deemed disposition tax entirely.

The final reason why this myth is indeed a myth is the fact that more often than not, the Canada-US Tax Treaty and the differential in US and Canadian domestic tax rules can be used to reduce or eliminate tax on unrealized gains that might need to be deferred in this CRA election. Taxes saved are always better than taxes deferred. If taxes cannot be easily saved, deferred taxes are better than paying taxes earlier than when they need to be paid. See section 2 of this chapter for a more in-depth discussion of this topic.

1.2 Subject to US estate taxes

The second myth this chartered accountant laid before his client was: "The US has an estate tax and, since your estate is very large, you would be subject to US estate taxes."

Two parts of this accountant's statement are actually true; there currently is a US estate tax and the client's estate is large. The myth part is client simply doesn't need to be subject to US estate tax in that all the client and his wife would have to do is set up one or more asset-protection or estate-planning trusts before they left Canada for the US. Whatever they put into the trust or trusts could be protected from US estate tax and other creditors. The trust protects assets gathered over a lifetime from creditors, including the CRA and the IRS, and at the same time eliminating or at least greatly reducing both US and Canadian estate taxes regardless of how large the estate grows and where the children or other beneficiaries live. (See section 3 for more details.)

1.3 Facing the Internal Revenue Service (IRS)

The third myth the trusted accountant said was, "You don't want to go to the US because you will have to face the IRS." This myth is harder to explain because the statement is actually true; it is just the insinuation that somehow dealing with the IRS is extremely bad or terrifying which perpetuates a myth. Yes, the IRS is no picnic to deal with but it is no different from dealing with any government agency including the CRA. Very simply, if you follow the rules, the IRS actually provides a much better set of taxpayer rights and systems to reconcile problems than the CRA.

The one thing that is different with the IRS when compared with the CRA, and this is where the IRS gets a lot of headlines, they will actually throw people in jail for fraudulently filing tax returns. I cannot remember the CRA throwing anyone in jail for underreporting income or other similar illegal practices. All the IRS has to do is put one person in jail for a particular item and all the others doing the same fraudulent activity are scared into compliance with the IRS rules.

If you follow the rules that taxpayers are obligated to follow, you will never have any significant problems with the IRS other than typical government bureaucracy such as not crediting a quarterly payment correctly or losing something in the mail. Following IRS rules is really no different or more complicated than following CRA rules since most taxpayers desire to follow the rules. If you follow IRS rules, it should pose no trouble for you when you are using the US as your chosen tax haven.

2. Dealing with the Canadian Departure Tax

The Canadian departure tax (also known as the exit tax), or deemed disposition tax on leaving the country is not an additional or a punitive tax, it is simply accelerating the time from when your assets would normally be sold by deeming them to be sold on the Canadian exit or moving date.

It would be nice to be able to say that the Canadian departure tax is much ado about nothing, but most Canadians give it a great deal of thought when considering moving or retiring to a tax haven, including the US Sun Belt. I believe the departure tax does get more attention than it deserves and many Canadian advisors are unaware of the tools available in the cross-border planning tool shed or incorrectly use it as a barrier or reason for their clients to not consider exiting.

Dealing with the departure tax can be complex. By understanding all of the issues in dealing with a cross-border move, clients can understand there are specialists available to assist them in achieving their goals in an accurate and expedited manner.

As most Canadian advisors and their clients understand, the departure tax is the tax that the CRA levies on a taxpayer's specified capital assets when he or she becomes a nonresident of Canada. The CRA requires that a taxpayer exiting Canada go through a deemed disposition or a deemed sale of certain assets on the date of departure. For tax purposes, under CRA rules, a deemed sale is always taxed as an actual sale of assets.

Canada taxes residents on their worldwide income only while they are actually living within its borders. Consequently, all you have to do is depart Canada and you will no longer be subject to Canadian tax rules. Canada's answer to this simplistic method of avoiding Canadian tax is to collect all the taxes due on any capital gains that have not yet been taxed prior to the taxpayer's departure, hence the departure tax. The best way to understand the departure tax is to understand what is not subject to the tax, since there are many myths and misunderstandings as to what is included in this tax.

The following is a list of assets that are not subject to any departure tax when moving from Canada:

1. Canadian real estate or resource properties.

2. Canadian business capital property (including inventory) if the business is carried on through a permanent establishment in Canada.

3. Pensions, all registered plans including RRSPs, registered retirement income funds, locked-in retirement accounts, tax-free savings accounts, retirement compensation arrangements, and deferred profit-sharing plans.

4. Employee stock options subject to tax in Canada.

5. Interest in life insurance policies or annuities in Canada.

6. Rights to certain benefits under employee profit-sharing plans, employee benefit plans, employee trusts, retirement allowances, and salary deferral arrangements.

7. Interests in certain trusts in which the trustee, trust control, and the trust assets will remain in Canada.

Now that we have looked at what is not subject to tax, it is a little bit easier to understand what is subject to the departure tax. This is the list of what is subject to departure tax:

1. All stocks (including closely held Canadian-controlled private corporations), bonds, mutual funds, exchange traded funds, limited or general partnership interests, and other similar securities that are not inside registered plans noted above in number 3.

2. US real estate and other foreign real estate.

3. Certain rights or interests in foreign trusts.

4. Personal property that has appreciated in value such as artwork or antiques.

If you compare the two lists as to what is and what isn't subject to departure tax, you can easily surmise a large number of Canadians would not be subject to any departure tax at all. Those Canadians who may be subject to departure tax have several options to mitigate, defer, or eliminate this tax altogether.

2.1 Defer or eliminate the departure tax

When Canadian residents move to the US, the CRA requires that they file exit tax returns for the year of their departure. This exit return is a regular T1 form filed by the April 30 deadline following the year of departure, with the exit date clearly indicated on the first page of the T1 and all the appropriate schedules, forms, and disclosures completed as required. The important forms to be filed with an exit T1 are Form T1161, "List of Properties by an Emigrant of Canada"; and Form T1243, "Deemed Disposition Property by an Emigrant of Canada," which lists and calculates the net capital gains on those owned items subject to the exit tax. Each property deemed to be disposed of is deemed to have been re-acquired by the individual at the time of emigration at a cost equal to the proceeds of the disposition of the property. Any capital gains tax due may be paid with the return or deferred using the procedures noted in the next paragraph.

To elect to defer this exit tax, the exiting taxpayer must complete and file Form T1244, "Defer the Payment of Tax on Income Relating to the Deemed Disposition of Property," with their exit tax return. They are required to post suitable security with the CRA equal to the tax due. The tax due need not be paid until the assets subject to the deemed disposition tax are actually sold.

It is important to realize that since the CRA charges no interest on the tax due, by electing to defer, the taxpayer is in exactly the same situation as if he or she stayed in Canada holding the same securities or properties. So why are so many emigrants overly concerned about leaving Canada and paying an exit tax? Unfortunately, all too often, concern with the exit tax is a result of not knowing the basic rules.

Using the election to defer taxes is just a worst-case scenario; there are many cross-border options to legitimately minimize or eliminate any exit tax that may be due. These options include, but are not limited to, the following:

- Most investment portfolios, at any given time, have some securities in a gain position and some in a loss position. When exiting, the taxpayer may offset the losses against gains and therefore be subject to tax only if there is net gain on the portfolio.

- Use the Canada-US Tax Treaty to eliminate the tax entirely on a net basis by turning the so-called exit tax into foreign tax credits, that can be used to reduce US income taxes on a dollar-for-dollar basis once the taxpayer has taken up residency in the US. This is a powerful tool in the cross-border planning tool shed to deal with this complex option available when Canadians move to the US with treaty protection that is not available if they go offshore to a tax haven island.

- Use the small-business capital gains exemption (for a married couple this could mean up to $1.6 million of tax-free capital gains and, with good planning, an additional $800,000 for each child).

- Utilize capital losses carried forward that may be available from previous investment losses or failed investments to offset taxable gains upon the deemed disposition exit tax of other assets.

- If a taxpayer's spouse is not emigrating from Canada with the taxpayer, the appreciated assets could be transferred to the spouse on a tax-free basis. As the exiting taxpayer, he or she would have no exit tax when he or she departed Canada. The Canada-US Tax Treaty tiebreaker rules apply separately to each spouse (as noted in Chapter 5). Although having one spouse resident in one country and the other in the US is technically achievable under the treaty it is generally not recommended as a long-term strategy because it is difficult to accomplish as there are many "t"s to cross and "i"s to dot on a continuing basis. However, for a short-term strategy, when one spouse can move to the US with a large income-producing investment portfolio while the other stays in Canada to clean up other tax issues or sell a business, it can be tax effective. This kind of strategy would never be available to Canadians choosing a traditional tax haven without Treaty protection, since having a spouse remaining in Canada is a significant tie under the CRA domestic rules.

- If the exiting taxpayer has any assets that are not deemed to be disposed of when he or she crosses the border, and that have a net loss built into them (e.g., a terrible real estate investment), he or she may elect to go through a deemed disposition of this property on his or her exit and use the loss to offset other capital gains that are subject to the exit tax.

2.2 Principal residence disposition on exit

If you did not sell, or you do not wish to sell, your Canadian principal residence before departing Canada, you need to be aware of some special rules under the Canada-US Tax Treaty that can help you reduce future capital gains tax on the sale of your Canadian home while you are a US resident. The Treaty will help you around this problem by making it appear, for tax purposes, that you purchased the Canadian home at its fair market value the day you entered the US, provided you file the appropriate Treaty election with your US tax return for that tax year. As a result, you are responsible to the IRS for gains on this property only from the date that you became a US resident. Note that this step-up in cost basis for the taxpayer's principal residence applies only to non-US citizens or non-green card holders.

Other capital property that is subject to the deemed disposition on exit from Canada may also get a new cost basis for US tax purposes equal to the fair market value of the property on the exit date. To receive the special tax treatment, you must file a treaty election Form 8833, "Treaty-Based Return Position Disclosure," with the US tax return for the year of departure from Canada. Upon exit from Canada, if you have not elected for the deemed disposition of your principal residence on your exit tax return, you may convert it to rental property or transfer it to a specially designed cross-border trust. This will step up to the Canadian cost basis on the ultimate sale of the property to further reduce possible capital gains taxes in Canada because you would have received the tax-free principal residence exemption had the residence been sold before your departure from Canada.

It is highly recommended that Canadians who keep their principal residences when moving to the US get a fair market appraisal just before leaving Canada, and keep it for future tax reference when making the treaty or other elections.

3. Eliminating US Estate Taxes

Another important issue for wealthy Canadians looking to exit Canada so they can escape Canadian taxes is the potential estate or inheritance taxes in the jurisdiction to which they are considering moving. The US does have an estate tax.

Possible US estate taxes are another major reason the US is often overlooked as a potential tax haven for high-net-worth Canadians. However, with the use of a good cross-border estate planning specialist prior to the exit date from Canada, the US estate tax, for the most part, may be entirely eliminated. Not only can the US estate tax be avoided with good cross-border planning, so too can the Canadian deemed disposition tax at death also be greatly reduced or eliminated if the taxpayer chooses to still hold Canadian real estate or other assets once he or she has exited Canada.

Necessity is often the mother of invention. Since there is a greater need for comprehensive estate planning in the US, a number of very good and proven techniques have been developed to help make management of US taxpayers' estates easier while they are alive and then provide for a smooth transition to their heirs at their deaths. Many of these techniques will work equally well for Canadians who become residents of the US and they can be used to cover assets remaining in Canada.

When a taxpayer is moving or contemplating a move to the US, cross-border estate planning needs to be a top priority because there are many complex issues that could lead to unnecessary estate settlement costs and death taxes if not addressed before residency in the US is taken. There are many incredible tools available in the cross-border estate planning toolbox to assist clients not only to avoid US estate taxes but also solve complex Canadian estate problems that otherwise could be very costly.

Normally the first matter of business in cross-border estate planning is doing a comparison of what a client's estate costs and what taxes are in Canada and in the US, to see if there is any advantage in either country. It is not very often in cross-border estate planning that I can state a general rule that applies in almost every case, but I can say that couples with estates of less than US $11 million have an unquestionable death tax advantage as residents of the US over Canada under current rules. Since there are spousal trusts in Canada and qualified domestic-marital deduction trusts in the US to permit the transfer of assets, tax free, between spouses, it is generally best to concentrate on estate tax and settlement costs at the death of the second spouse, to measure the full impact of these costs and make a proper Canada-US comparison.

When comparing the US and Canadian estate taxes, many Canadian accountants, financial planners, and attorneys are quick to pontificate that Canada does not have an estate tax. Just because the CRA does not call the tax at death an "estate tax," it doesn't mean that most Canadians won't face a much higher estate tax in Canada than US residents who own similar-sized estates. Even if there are no other taxes or other personal objectives, eliminating the Canadian deemed disposition tax at death could be reason enough to look at moving to the US or other tax havens.

The IRS does not try to disguise its estate tax, and because of the high exemptions allowed, less than 1 percent of all US residents are subject to an estate tax. Consequently, US estate taxes are not a concern for most people in Canada and in the US.

A Canadian couple with an estate of $11 million would likely have a very large RRSP or other registered plan and highly appreciated investments or businesses which in total could easily produce Canadian deemed disposition taxes; in other words, estate or death taxes. For example a large RRSP with the value at death of $2 million will create Canadian death taxes in excess of $1 million when the second spouse dies. If this couple took up residence in the US and had a similar asset mix at the time of death, they could have absolutely no US or Canadian estate taxes due. Because the total size of their estate would be less than their combined total of US $11 million, US estate tax exemptions would totally shield them from US state taxes. This couple could deal with their RRSPs, as noted in Chapter 8, to get them out of Canada with no or very low income taxes on a net basis. In addition, the beneficiaries of the estate from the US residents would receive a free step-up in basis, without deemed disposition taxes, on any appreciated assets in the estate which simply means that all appreciated assets at the death of US citizens or residents can be sold without capital gains tax immediately after the deceased passing.

3.1 No Canadian Estate Tax Holiday

In Canada there is no tax-free holiday for beneficiaries of an estate (as there are for beneficiaries of US residents) so all deemed disposition taxes at death need to be paid before the beneficiaries can receive their inheritance. The Canadian deemed disposition tax on death is due by April 30 of the following year after death for those who died January 1 through October 31, or within six months after date of death for those that died November 1 through December 31. If the beneficiary is a surviving spouse, he or she can defer, but not reduce or eliminate, this deemed death tax until he or she sells the appreciated asset or cashes in the RRSP or RRIF or dies.

This major difference in leaving highly appreciated assets to a spouse or other beneficiary is best illustrated by showing what could happen if Bill Gates died tomorrow. It is estimated that Gates owns about $60 billion dollars of Microsoft stock. Under US estate rules, if he died and left all his stock to his wife and/or children, she or they could turn around and sell all of this stock with zero income tax. Whereas, if Gates was a resident of Canada with the same $60 billion of appreciated stock, there would be capital gains tax due to the CRA of about $15 billion if his wife or children sold the stock. (If Gates' wife was in Canada and inherited all of the stock she could choose not to sell the stock; the $15 billion tax would still be payable any time during her life on a full or partial sell, or all would be due at her death.)

3.2 Pre-US-entry trust

For estates of more than $11 million USD per couple, or $5.5 million USD for individuals, other US estate-planning techniques can be used to deal economically with almost any size estate or estate tax liability. A primary recommended tool in the cross-border estate planning tool shed for Canadians coming to the US with an estate exceeding their US estate-tax exemption amounts is to set up or settle a trust or series of trusts prior to becoming subject to the US estate-tax rules. These trusts are often called Dynasty Trusts because they can span multiple generations of each family and last as long as family desires, contrast this to the typical Canadian estate planning Trusts which are normally liquidated after just 21 years to pay capital gains tax all of the appreciated assets due to the CRA deemed disposition rule on the 21st year. Not only can these trusts achieve all of their personal estate goals but at the same time they can provide living benefits such as income or use of assets from the trust for the balance of the trust creators' lives and also those of their beneficiaries for several generations. Another benefit is if these Dynasty Trusts have been drafted properly, they provide creditor protection of the family assets throughout generations to protect family assets from divorces and bankruptcies in perpetuity if necessary or until the trust assets are expended by the trust creators and beneficiaries.

Wealthy Canadians who become US residents and are concerned about leaving a larger estate for beneficiaries may use some or all income tax savings from their reduced tax burden, by moving to the US to purchase life insurance inside specially designed trusts. This type of planning can provide a nice tax-free legacy for family or other chosen beneficiaries.

The complexity of these issues underscores the necessity of consulting with a cross-border financial planning specialist to ensure clients maximize the opportunities and minimize the pitfalls of cross-border estate planning.

4. Immigration to a Tax Haven

To become a legal resident of a traditional island tax haven, you must generally meet that country's financial requirement such as purchasing a home of a certain dollar value or investing a minimum sum in one of the local banks, along with spending a minimum amount of time there to qualify. Very few traditional tax havens ever allow outsiders to become citizens; this requires that the Canadians maintain some ties to Canada to keep their passports current.

There are normally two legal ways to immigrate to the US. The first is through a business or a professional relationship. The second is through the sponsorship of a close family member. There may possibly be a third way to immigrate to the US due to a pending US immigration law (discussed in section 4.4). Within these two broad family and business categories, there are numerous options available to Canadians. The number of combinations and permutations as a result of all these options can get very confusing and seem quite complex. In this section I will outline only a few of the family and business immigration options to illustrate the ease at which US immigration can be obtained by those who like to use the US as their tax haven.

The following sections offer a general discussion of American immigration rules and policies. Individual factors can greatly influence the course of any immigration undertaking. Immigration can be a complex and lengthy procedure under current law and should not be attempted without the services of a good US immigration attorney.

4.1 North American Free Trade Agreement (NAFTA)

The North American Free Trade Agreement (NAFTA), since it came into existence in the early 1990s, provides a variety of visas with allowances for a few days to a few months for a Canadian citizen. However, these visas are nonimmigrant visas that must be renewed periodically and some can be renewed only a certain number of times; it all depends on the type of visa obtained. None of these visas can be used to obtain US citizenship, so for someone attempting to live permanently in the US for long-term tax benefits, he or she should use this visa only as a temporary bridge to obtaining Legal Permanent Status (LPR) or so-called green card status. Green card status is the Holy Grail for Canadians wishing to live permanently in the US and eventually become dual citizens of Canada and the US.

Once a green card is obtained, a Canadian is eligible for US citizenship after five years (three years if the green card was obtained through marriage to a US citizen). Those who have recently retired or are about to retire should consider keeping open any business or professional relationships long enough to assist them in getting permanent immigration status. For those who are retired, investing in a small US business with a full-time manager or just a US Citizenship and Immigration Services (USCIS) specially authorized investment can be a suitable means of obtaining a visa or legal permanent resident card that allows them to live legally in the US year-round.

4.2 The gold card

For those who have sold their businesses and have no desire to be involved in business directly there is one green card opportunity that is relatively easy for wealthy Canadians to obtain permanent US status. I generally refer to this green card opportunity for Canadians as the "gold card." This permanent resident status option is technically referred to as the USCIS employment-based EB-5 Immigrant Investor Program.

This immigrant investor program is similar to the program Canada has used for years to attract foreign business entrepreneurs. In 2002, the USCIS introduced an EB-5 Regional Center Program, which is ideal for the retiree or inactive investor who wishes to immigrate to the US. This EB-5 program provides a Conditional Lawful Permanent Residence (i.e., a conditional green card) for two years until all the requirements listed below are met; then full green card or LPR status is granted.

The required investment amount for the EB-5 Regional Center Program is $500,000 invested in the targeted areas of high unemployment or areas of desired economic expansion as preapproved by the EB-5 Regional Center Program. The regional program the immigrant investor subscribes to must prove that, as a result of the investment, at least ten indirect jobs were created. The investor can qualify by presenting evidence that ten jobs will be created throughout the EB-5 Regional Center economy. This proof is provided for the EB-5 investor by the regional center sponsor and is a relatively easy hurdle to face for the experienced program sponsor. The EB-5 management requirement is nil in that the investor can be a limited or silent partner and still qualify, making this program much more acceptable for those who are not interested in day-to-day management or actively running a business. The investor is not required to live where the investment is made; for example, he or she can live in Florida and invest in Washington. Married couples need only have one of the spouses make the $500,000 investment and apply and the other spouse automatically obtains his or her green card in the same fashion under this EB-5 program.

There are currently more than 150 EB-5 Regional Center Programs for the investor to choose from. Thus, the only major concern for an investor is to choose the right investment, the program managers do the rest. After approximately ten months, the investor has his or her conditional two-year green card. At the end of the two years, the green card becomes permanent with full rights of permanent residency and a path to US citizenship. The investment can be sold at any time after the permanent green card has been obtained; in fact, most of these investments self-liquidate in five to seven years after inception and can be maintained more or less on a permanent basis. Choosing the right investment cannot be overemphasized, as the program should give investors a fair return on their investment, and the green card should be considered a secondary benefit or just the icing on the cake.

Under mandate by Congress, EB-5 Regional Center petitions are given priority by USCIS, which, among other benefits, often results in a quicker path to approval. We have seen some EB-5 applicants obtain their green card in as little as three months, but on average it takes about eight months, while others have a green card within twelve or more months. It all depends on how organized the Regional Center sponsor is and the workload of the USCIS center where the EB-5 application is processed.

The procedure for obtaining an EB-5 investor green card is relatively straightforward. The investor must produce five years of tax returns to substantiate the legal source of investment funds. The source of the funds can also be in the form of a loan or gift from a friend or relative. The investor must also present evidence that traces the capital, through bank transfers and other documentation, from the investor directly to the enterprise being invested in.

If the investor is already in the US, he or she then applies for a green card through US Citizenship and Immigration Services (USCIS). Customarily no interview is required, and approval has been taking approximately ten months.

If the investor still lives in Canada, an application for the green card is generally made at a US consulate; however, for consular processing purposes, an interview is necessary which means a trip to Montreal. Approval of the green card in this case takes an average of about ten or eleven months, approximately the same as directly through USCIS.

4.3 Family immigration sponsorship

In the US, the family sponsorship programs for green cards come from having US citizen parents, children, siblings, or spouses. In some cases, having US citizen grandparents can be of help. Depending on the relationship to the green card applicant, it can take from a few months to several years to get a green card through a family member sponsorship. This is an extremely desirable method for immigration to the US when it is available because of its low cost and relative simplicity.

4.4 Pending retirement visa

In 2013 the US Senate passed a comprehensive immigration bill that included in it provisions for Canadian snowbirds to apply for a visa that would allow them to stay up to 365 days a year in the US. This bill has yet to be voted on by the House of Representatives so therefore it continues to languish and will need to be reintroduced in the new Congress that was elected in the November 2014 midterm elections.

Because of the politics behind this major immigration bill the Canadian part of it just has to go along with the more politically sensitive parts of the legislation and I suspect these will be debated for several more years before being voted on again. The retirement visa would allow Canadians to spend 365 days a year in the US if they desired, but permission to work would not be authorized under the terms of the visa. In addition, this visa would not allow Canadians to become dual citizens or permanent residents; they would still need to obtain legal permanent resident or green card status. Many Canadians looking at using the US as a tax haven already have one or more US residences and have no desire to work in the US.

The visa, once it is passed into law, could be an excellent vehicle for a very quick entry to the US and/or a bridge to applying for a green card through one of the other programs such as the EB-5 program noted in section **4.2**.

If you are interested in this bill, write to Senators and congressional representatives in your area of influence to encourage them to pass the bill as soon as possible, emphasizing the fact that this would be a job creation bill for the US. I am hoping this will be passed in 2015 but realistically we could be waiting several more years to see it brought into law.

10

Choosing the Best Advisors for the Job

It is important to understand that the old saying "you don't know what you don't know" applies in full force when establishing a plan for a lifestyle in the US Sun Belt. The complexities associated with this planning are wrought with minefields such that those attempting to do it on their own or with the advice of untrained or inexperienced advisors will surely step into costly mistakes. In most instances, proper cross-border planning should not be conducted without the full guidance of experienced and trained professionals that know of all the tools in the cross-border planning toolbox and how to apply them efficiently in a timely manner.

With my years of experience in assisting families with the complexity of a cross-border lifestyle, we, at KeatsConnelly, have developed an extremely thorough and efficient, scalable process to assist families to enhance their cross-border lifestyle and provide substantial income tax relief from what I believe is the best tax haven for Canadians, the United States of America. I will outline this well-established cross-border financial-planning process so that you will have a number of important takeaways:

- You will have a better understanding of the complexities and the scope of the cross-border planning process.

- You will have a measuring tool and checklist to question any advisor you are talking with to ensure he or she covers all the different aspects and he or she has the amount and depth of experience necessary for you to benefit from the best lifestyle and tax savings choices in line with your goals.

- If you do want to use the services of a specialty cross-border planning firm, you will have familiarity with the process so the chances of your expectations being met are greatly improved.

1. The Four Phases of Cross-Border Planning

The four phases of cross-border planning include data gathering, a pre-exit plan, a post-exit plan, and maintenance. It is extremely important that the majority of the work and the entire amount of coordination of any outside professional expertise required be integrated and coordinated with the plan in all four phases. It can be extremely stressful and time consuming for anyone wishing to move cross-border to attempt to coordinate all of the many details and professionals without the assistance of an experienced team who can get the job done easily and in a timely fashion. Specialists in this area can make these kinds of dreams come true with minimal hassle and can move families to the enjoyment phase quickly, profitably, and judiciously. As with most things in life, professionals make difficult things look easy, whether it be in hockey, brain surgery, or cross-border financial planning!

1.1 Data gathering

In order to gather data, your cross-border financial planner will need to establish a complete baseline of your family's goals, objectives, and financial picture. The planner will need to get the exact details of the family as a whole and the individual family member goals everyone would like to achieve. All planning must be focused to assist you and your family to achieve these goals.

In addition, the data-gathering phase provides a comprehensive profile of every specific asset and income source you have or will have in the future to identify tax benefits, cash-flow needs, and develop planning opportunities.

This phase is what I consider the "pre-drilling phase" (borrowing from the universe of drilling for oil). If you had a piece of land that may have prospects for a productive oil well, you wouldn't just go out and start punching holes in the ground at $10 million a hole. You would normally hire geologists and geophysicists to do seismic and geology work to determine the probability of a successful oil well and tell you the best places to drill, or possibly not to drill at all because the success probabilities are bleak. If your prospects for drilling are very bleak, you should not consider the money invested in the seismic work as a loss but as huge savings of the drilling expense and dry hole frustration. Similarly, at the end of the data-gathering phase of the cross-border plan, any potential plan-destroying obstacles can be identified, costs of implementation estimated, as well as any perspective tax or cost-of-living savings calculated so that time and money is not wasted, and the opportunities can be exploited to the highest degree in the other phases of the cross-border planning.

1.2 The pre-exit plan

Once the data-gathering phase is complete and there is a green light to continue the cross-border planning process, there are a myriad of details you need to deal with and plan around in all areas of your affairs prior to emigrating from Canada. It is critical that most of these items are completed prior to becoming a US taxpayer.

Incredible tax savings may be revealed as well potential tax traps by covering and coordinating all the different areas of the pre-exit plan with respect to RRSPs, corporations, real estate, estate planning, investments, medical coverage, and immigration. Each of these areas of your finances were covered in great detail throughout this book. In particular, review the areas about avoiding the Canadian exit tax, reducing the tax on RRSPs, avoiding the US estate tax, and the sale of a Canadian business at very low tax rates.

In the pre-exit phase of the plan, the best US state to achieve your lifestyle and tax goals can be determined. The success of your tax results can vary greatly based on your chosen state of residence.

1.3 The post-exit plan

Once the pre-exit planning has been implemented and the immigration process completed, you are a US resident and taxpayer. There are a number of very important steps that need to be carried out now that you are no longer a Canadian taxpayer. As a nonresident of Canada, you are eligible to receive Canada-US Tax Treaty benefits.

Several of these post-exit items will be unwinding planning items from the pre-exit phase at the Canada-US Tax Treaty rates and a much lower tax rate than if you were still a resident of Canada.

Also, because you are now a resident of a new country with full immigration and tax status, remaining items such as applying for a Social Security Number, driver's license, and creating a new will need to be established in your official state of residence.

1.4 Maintenance

Maintenance is the "enjoyment phase" of the cross-border lifestyle. This phase, as the name depicts, is the routine task of looking after all the details which optimize and realize the substantial benefits of the planning conducted in the first three phases. The majority of these tasks are annual or more frequent reviews to report on or an update on the progress of a family's improvement toward the goals identified in the data-gathering phase noted in section 1.1. Annual tax planning and tax return filing, investment management, and periodic updates to estate plans are all part of the maintenance phase.

This phase should be designed to be flexible so that it is easily adjusted to assist the family in life transitions such as a death in the family, a divorce, the education of children or grandchildren, and any changes in family goals or desires.

In addition, this phase of the planning process keeps all access and doors open to Canada if you choose to travel and spend time in Canada or even if you wish to return entirely at some point in the future without jeopardizing any of the lifestyle choices of living in a warmer climate and re-optimizing tax planning.

The Milestone Diagram in Sample 18 depicts each of these four phases along with a summary of the workings and general goals of each phase.

2. The Dually Qualified Planning Professional

Whom should you seek as your team leader to assist you most effectively to use the US as your cross-border lifestyle choice and to use the US as your tax haven? I believe it is appropriate at this point to explain the ideal cross-border planning professional.

Canada and the US (as well as more than 60,000 individuals in 30 countries throughout the world) have a professional designation for financial planners that is considered the premier world standard. This designation is the Certified Financial Planner® (CFP®).

Each country that uses the CFP certification for planners conducts their own accreditation and supervision of their CFP applicants based on the unique requirements of the original CFP board in the US. Because of the widespread acceptance, high standards, and disciplinary enforcement of its qualified members, the CFP professional designation now has growing worldwide recognition as being the financial planning certification for consumers to seek for professional assistance with their financial planning needs.

To become a CFP an individual must meet the following basic standards separately in each country or countries he or she chooses to operate or provide advice within (these requirements vary slightly by country):

- A fully accredited bachelor's college degree.

- Pass a series of at least six individual courses available through numerous college and universities approved by the CFP board. These courses are designed in order that the student master a minimum of 100 integrated financial planning topics covering taxation, investment, risk management and insurance, employee benefits, estate planning, retirement planning, and general principles of financial planning.

- Pass a ten-hour certification exam over a two-day examination period. This comprehensive exam is usually the sixth and final course requirement noted in the previous bullet point.

- Obtain a minimum of three years' experience directly related to the financial planning profession.

- Subscribe to and agree to follow a very comprehensive CFP Code of Ethics and Professional Responsibility, which puts clients' interests first, and comply with the Financial Planning Practice Standards which spell out what clients should be able to reasonably expect from the financial planning engagement. These standards include agreement by the planning professional to be disciplined by the CFP board for violations of the Code of Ethics.

- Once CFP certification is approved by the board, the CFP professional must maintain a minimum of 30 hours of approved financial planning continuing education credits every two years as well as pay an annual certification fee.

The ideal professional to lead the team necessary to accomplish a complete cross-border financial plan is a professional who invested the time, cost, and ongoing continuing education to obtain and maintain both the Canadian CFP and the US CFP designations. I believe this dual qualification, although rare, is the minimum specialist credentials necessary for leading the most successful cross-border lifestyle and tax haven move and consumers should demand no less.

3. Dually Qualified Team Members

Other very helpful professionals that make very good members or assistant team leaders of the cross-border planning team are accountants who are dually (Canada and US) qualified and have both the Canadian Chartered Public Accountant (CPA) and the US Certified Public Accountant (CPA) designations.

Lawyers who are admitted to the bar in both Canada and the US in tax, estate planning, and immigration also make very good team members. However, because accountants and lawyers have a very narrow area of focus and expertise, they generally lack the comprehensive interdisciplinary skills needed to coordinate all the different areas of expertise that those with the dual CFP certification are able to cover because they are trained in the basics of all the disciplines. For example, accountants and lawyers, unless also qualified as a CFP certificant or with similar training, know very little about investment management, health and other insurance requirements, and general financial planning principles, which are all critical requirements for a successful cross-border move. Whereas a dually qualified CFP professional would have a general knowledge of the tax, accounting, and legal requirements for a cross-border move in addition to the experience and skills to know what tools are available in the cross-border planning toolbox and then using or assisting the use of the tools to solve problems or create opportunities. These specialized tools would be missing or at least unrecognized when using only accountants or lawyers.

4. Chartered Public Accountants (CPAs) in Canada and Certified Public Accountants (CPAs) in the US

Many people assume that Chartered Public Accountants (CPAs) in Canada and Certified Public Accountants (CPAs) in the US are qualified to do financial planning. While Canadian CPAs and US CPAs are skilled in preparing personal or corporate financial statements, and some are generally qualified to give tax advice in their own country, problems arise when it comes to investment selection, immigration planning, insurance counseling, and estate planning in one or both countries. To optimize your full transition to your enriched cross-border lifestyle, all these important subjects must be professionally coordinated on a cross-border basis, or serious consequences and missed opportunities may result. Professional accountants, by training and temperament, are neither investment counselors nor estate planners, nor do they generally have a good working knowledge of insurance matters. Even though your Canadian accountant may have been your trusted advisor for many years, it is both unrealistic and unfair for you to ask this person to provide cross-border financial-planning services.

Some of the most outrageous adverse tax situations I have seen in the cross-border financial planning structures were set up by Canadian accounting firms big and small. Due to their lack of cross-border planning experience, these accountants often structure US businesses like Canadian businesses and this most frequently costs clients thousands or even hundreds of thousands of dollars in unnecessary taxes annually.

Professional accountants can make excellent cross-border financial planning team members, but because of their narrow focus they are not always suitable as team leaders. For that role, you need the dually qualified CFP Certified Financial Planner (US and Canada) professional who can coordinate and implement all the immigration, tax, insurance, risk management, estate, and investment issues necessary for a cross-border plan.

5. What to Expect from Cross-Border Financial Planners

The majority of the public have never heard of or dealt with a cross-border financial-planning professional, practitioner, or expert. As a result, they have no concept of what it entails or what they should expect. By reading this far in this book, you should now have a good grasp of the number and complexity of problems you'll encounter in preparing any good cross-border financial plan. The sheer number of possibilities can be overwhelming. Missing just one opportunity or doing one step incorrectly or in the wrong order can be extremely costly to you.

A professional, dually qualified cross-border financial-planning practitioner, CFP (US and Canada), can very quickly sort through rules and regulations, and very expeditiously tell you which rules apply to your situation, and how to incorporate them into your planning objectives.

milestone diagram

Financial Planning Process

Data Gathering Phase

Pre-Exit Phase

- Planning team assigned.
- Expectations/Introductory phone call.
- Client completes detailed life-plan questionnaire.
- Client submits copies of all requested documents.
- Goals and Objectives (G&O) meeting with client to gain deeper understanding of goals, needs, and values.
- Financial and nonfinancial assumptions documented.
- Financial projections developed.
- Client reviews, corrects, and approves of G&Os (financial and nonfinancial) and financial data (assumptions, net worth, and cashflow statements).

- Planning team analyzes data and develops recommendations that address client's G&Os.
- Planning team develops pre-exit & post-exit planning analysis and action checklists.
- Planner presents plan to client linking plan to client's goals, needs, and values.
- Client approves or rejects pre-exit plan.

 - This symbol indicates milestones with deliverables. It also indicates discrete points in time that generally separate sequential activities.

Post-Exit Phase

Maintenance Phase

- Planning team and client work together implementing client-approved pre-exit plan.
- Client immigrates to the US.
- Planning team and client work together implementing post-exit plan.
- Client establishes full US residency and implements US new resident checklist and estate plan.

- Planning team performs quarterly reviews and re-balancing of portfolio.
- Client keeps planning team informed of any major changes in family circumstances or goals.
- Planning team conducts reviews and plans updates, as required, to ensure client is on track to meet his or her objectives by linking the plan to client's goals, needs, and values.

Expect a written plan that will address your concerns, along with a detailed analysis with specific recommendations. The cross-border plan when moving to the US should:

- Determine which tools in the cross-border planning tool shed to use along with when and how they will be applied in your precise situation to achieve your specific goals.

- Tell you how each of your assets will be taxed by either country, before and after leaving Canada, your current country of residence.

- Show you the best way to keep residences in both Canada and the US and to spend time in each country without adverse tax or immigration consequences.

- Provide a Canadian or US net worth and cash-flow statement.

- Provide detailed tax projections of the tax options available to you, both personally and for businesses.

- Provide a risk-management and creditor-protection plan to help safeguard you from any financial disasters in medical or liability expenses.

- Provide a complete cross-border estate plan that looks after all of your assets, whether they are located in Canada or the US (or both countries), and take into account who your beneficiaries are, their financial acumen or lack thereof, their marital status, and where they are located, as well as what your personal desires are.

- Provide a complete investment program that takes into consideration your income needs, your tax bracket, your risk tolerance, the location of and the ability to turn your assets readily into cash, and the size of your estate (this should not be confused with purchasing investments from your planner; I believe you will get the best advice from a planner who does not earn commissions or other transaction type fees from the investments he or she recommends for you).

- Provide a retirement and benefit plan to maximize pensions, CPP or QPP, OAS, and US Social Security benefits, and ensure your income and assets are not depleted during you and your spouse's lifetimes.

- Provide you with complete recommendations for how to maintain your business properly or sell it for optimum benefits.

Clear and easy-to-understand oral and written communications are imperative. Nothing is more frustrating than hiring a technically competent professional and then not being able to understand his or her directions. Developing a good rapport with any professional individual or team you hire is critical, in order that a fair and open exchange of ideas takes place. If you do not feel comfortable with the person you are considering as your planner, address it up front or seek another person for the job, perhaps even someone else at the same firm.

6. What Does Your Cross-Border Lifestyle Dream Cost?

There is mostly good news in this category, as in the majority of cases a good dually qualified and experienced Certified Financial Planner (US and Canada) professional can save you substantially more in taxes, commissions, and fees than what you are currently paying. Besides getting the cross-border lifestyle you desire, you can have considerably more after-tax income to spend after all professional fees are paid. You can make a nice profit both in one-time savings and ongoing annual savings on such items as the following:

- Income taxes.
- Cost-of-living expenses.
- Lower management fees and commissions on investments.
- Avoiding the goods and service tax (GST or HST).
- Lower estate taxes and settlement costs.

Any one or any combination of the above items can allow you to have your cake and eat it too, which is a better chosen lifestyle and more disposable income for the rest of your life and/or a larger estate to pass on to your chosen beneficiaries.

6.1 How are cross-border financial planners compensated?

Financial planners in either Canada or the US are compensated by four key methods:

- Retainer or hourly fee.
- Commission.
- A combination of fee and commission.
- Salary.

If you are dealing with a professional financial planner, he or she should provide you with a full written disclosure of the amounts of all fees or commissions you will be charged and the method by which he or she is compensated for his or her services. If this information was not voluntarily provided, make certain you ask for full disclosure or avoid using him or her altogether.

In addition to considering a dually qualified CFP (US and Canada) professional who is in full compliance with both the Canadian and US respective CFP boards, other professional organization planners can or should become members to add credibility and enhance consumer protection. It is desirable that your cross-border planner be a member of a well-established Canadian and US professional organizations such as the Institute of Advanced Financial Planners (IAFP) in Canada, the Financial Planning Association (FPA) in the US, or the National Association of Personal Financial Advisors (NAPFA) in the US. To varying degrees these professional organizations have codes of ethics that require that planners provide clients with full disclosure of how they are compensated before any engagement.

Planners who take all or part of their compensation through commissions seem to have the hardest time disclosing what they and their firms are taking as direct or indirect commissions: trips to exotic places as sales incentives, price spreads or markups on security trades, and trail or residual commission payments. These commissions and incentives are quite complicated and can be easily hidden, so buyer beware.

Which method of compensation is best for the clients is the subject of much debate. As a cross-border financial planning professional, I have found that most clients prefer their cross-border professional to be compensated on a fee-only basis. They find it reassuring to know that they do not have to buy any financial products to get the necessary advice and that there are no hidden costs or undesirable motives from their planners. Since other cross-border financial planning team members such as accountants and lawyers are usually compensated by fees for their services, there is often a better rapport between the team members if the cross-border financial planner or team leader is paid the same way. There are far too many potential areas of conflict of interest if your cross-border planner, particularly the team leader, is compensated either fully or partially on commissions, no matter how hard he or she may try to convince you otherwise. Commissioned salespeople or brokers are more transaction- and less planning-orientated when the cross-border team needs to be concentrating on the details of planning rather than selling products.

Regardless of how you pay for your cross-border financial plan, a good general rule, as with most things, is that you get what you pay for. A budget plan could get you budget results and may end up costing you thousands of dollars more in lost benefits, higher-than-necessary taxes, and less than optimal investment results. A cross-border financial planning analysis is much too complex an endeavor to take chances by cutting corners. Hiring a cheap cross-border financial planner is like hiring a cheap brain surgeon. Your results may be disastrous and irreversible if done incorrectly. Consider the fee you are paying as an investment and expect a return on that investment. You should find that a good cross-border plan is substantially more expensive than a domestic plan but it typically offers you many more opportunities for an enriched cross-border lifestyle and a much greater return on your investment than the basic domestic planners on either side of the border.

You can expect a cross-border financial-planning assessment from an experienced, fee-only planner to require a minimum fee depending on the experience and credentials of the individual or firm hired. Depending on the size and complexity of your estate, many plans can cost more than $100,000, but they can be worth every penny and provide you one of the best returns on investment that you may make anywhere. These fees are normally totally or partially tax-deductible either in Canada or the US or both so the net out-of-pocket expense can be cut by a third to a half.

A complete cross-border financial planning analysis normally takes hundreds of hours to complete adequately and can include many vital pages of analysis and recommendations. Implementation of the plan takes an equal or greater amount of professional assistance, so it is often best to get a planner who will include both the planning and the implementation in one all-encompassing fee.

Once the cross-border financial planning analysis has been completed and implemented, there are usually ongoing costs to maintain the plan, manage investment portfolios, update estate documentation, and prepare tax returns.

Generally, legal and accounting fees for implementation are provided under coordination with outside professionals and these outside costs are generally not included in the cross-border planning fee by the dually qualified CFP professional and team. However, your cross-border planner can negotiate on your behalf to minimize these outside costs.

6.2 Putting costs into perspective

To put the cost of a cross-border financial-planning analysis into perspective, it is useful to compare it to other financial transactions such as investment-portfolio management or the purchase of a house. In Chapter 3, Samples 1 and 3, I provided some typical costs and superior after-tax, after-fee returns on a basic $10 million investment portfolio for someone using the US as his or her tax haven.

Regardless of whether your portfolio is substantially smaller or larger, the average cost of managing a portfolio in Canada is generally around 2 percent and it's around 1 percent in the US. In Chapter 3 I also exposed a lot of the hidden costs and the undisclosed costs of portfolio management. Consequently, if you have a typical portfolio arrangement in Canada and you are paying close to 2 percent in both disclosed and hidden or undisclosed costs (as noted in Chapter 3 it is very often the case with the bigger banks and brokerage firms that only about half of the fees the client pays are fully disclosed, hopefully the new disclosure rules in Canada will shine a light on the undisclosed fees), it is costing you around $200,000 per year out of pocket to manage a $10 million portfolio.

A full cross-border planning analysis from a dually qualified CFP professional must include portfolio management for optimal results. Even though the cross-border analysis is substantially more complex and requires a much higher level of professional expertise and manpower to complete and maintain, it can normally be done for less than the standard Canadian portfolio management fees which a consumer is already paying or will be paying if he or she remains in Canada.

For example, another way to put the cost of a cross-border plan in perspective: If you were to purchase a home in the US for $500,000, you would pay real estate agent commissions and other expenses totaling close to $35,000. For that $35,000, you utilize anywhere from a few hours to a few weekends of the realtor's time. That particular realtor may have had very little experience or training and may have just been recently licensed. Once you own the home you have to pay for annual maintenance, taxes, and insurance costs. Cross-border financial-planning analyses are a bargain compared to those kinds of financial transactions for the following reasons:

- From years of experience as a cross-border financial-planning professional I have found that it takes anywhere from 150 to 700 hours to complete and implement a proper cross-border financial-planning analysis for a client, depending on the complexity of the client's financial situation and goals.

- The persons putting together a cross-border plan should have a high degree of technical training, licensing, certifications, and many years of experience in both Canada and the US.

- The cross-border financial-planning analysis may save you many times its initial costs in tax savings, lower investment costs, better access to medical professionals or facilities, and a more enjoyable retirement and lifestyle. In general, a target that I like to set in a cross-border plan is that, in the first five years, total savings of taxes, fees, commissions, and other benefits should be five times or more that of the actual investment in the cost of the cross-border financial-planning analysis.

- Purchasing an additional home is more likely to be an added expense and it will not save you money or give you additional benefits other than providing another place to live. Hopefully, there may be some profit when you eventually sell the home.

- You may purchase several houses during your lifetime but you are likely to only need one cross-border financial-planning analysis.

- A cross-border financial-planning analysis can not only make your retirement life more enjoyable but it can actually substantially reduce or even eliminate the risk of running out of money in retirement.

6.3 A value proposition

The bottom line in a cross-border financial-planning analysis is: Does it create value for you? Value is often very subjective and can mean many things to different people. For example, some people might consider that value is just being able to have the cross-border lifestyle that they desire, while others would like to see value that can be measured in dollars and cents.

Would you invest $100,000 in a plan that would save you $1 million in income taxes and offer a lower cost of living? Most people, including myself, would jump at the chance to get that kind of return on an investment. However, over the years I have seen many people turn down that opportunity just because they have never paid any professional accountant, attorney, or financial planner that amount of money for any reason in their entire lives. Therefore, based on principle alone, they will not make such an investment, regardless of the logic.

Cross-border financial-planning professionals can usually provide assurances that their work will achieve tax or other savings in excess of their fees. Ask for this type of commitment from your chosen planner before you initiate an engagement.

The highest paid member of the cross-border financial planning team should be the one who can save you the most money and, in most cases, that would be the dually qualified CFP (US and Canada), team leader and cross-border financial-planning professional.

7. Tips on Finding the Best Cross-Border Financial Planner

The following tips will help you find the best cross-border financial planner to help you realize your preferred lifestyle dreams:

- If you ask your long-time accountant or lawyer for recommendations on finding a professional cross-border financial planner, he or she is most likely going to refer you to someone in his or her own firm or close network, rather the best person for the job.

- Just because you know and trust your long-time accountant or lawyer it is not reasonable to expect him or her to be able to assist you with the complex multi-disciplinary planning and implementation of a cross-border move. However, these long-term trusted advisors are invaluable to provide baseline tax information and historical data that is of great importance to the cross-border financial planning professional.

- The accountants' and lawyers' respective codes of conduct require them to disclose to you their lack of qualification, knowledge, or experience in providing you the advice you seek and need.

- The so-called specialist your accountant or lawyer refers you to may not be a dually qualified professional in cross-border planning, which means he or she won't cover all the bases you absolutely need covered and he or she may have to refer you to a second specialist with whom someone (likely you) will need to coordinate.

- Two singly qualified specialists (for example a Canadian Chartered Personal Accountant along with a US Certified Public Accountant) are unlikely to refer you to a particular professional who is dually qualified in both specialties needed, so that they may earn fees for themselves and protect their turf, not to mention potentially doubling your costs.

- A dually qualified specialist in cross-border financial planning is going to know shortcuts and many tricks of the trade that single-specialty advisors just don't know or understand. They know the tools available in the cross-border planning tool shed and how to use them most effectively.

- If you can find a dually qualified specialist, you can make your life substantially easier, save money, and are most likely going to have a better outcome.

- If something is not completed correctly, having one advisor to hold responsible, although unpleasant, is much easier to deal with than getting in the middle of finger-pointing arguments between two separately qualified professionals — possibly one in Canada and one in the US.

It takes considerable additional time and cost for a professional to become a dually qualified specialist, therefore, very few professionals make the effort. Consequently, finding a dually qualified specialist does take extra research and effort and often requires you to bypass your current accountant or lawyer. However, once located, the dually qualified specialist can actually be a time-saver, a considerable cost reducer, and a provider of improved tax benefits on top of providing you a smoother and more solid base to transition to your new chosen lifestyle.

8. The Next Step to Your Enriched Cross-Border Lifestyle

Now that you have finished reading this book, you should have answered the question of whether or not a cross-border lifestyle using the US as a tax haven is desirable and obtainable for you and your family. You should now seek your dually qualified CFP (US and Canada) to get your planning started.

If you are still not certain, please don't hesitate to contact me and I can guide you through a complete review of your situation. If you have still not made a final decision, KeatsConnelly can assist you with a simple analysis. For a very basic fee to cover our out-of-pocket costs, we can give you a high-level assessment to help you make a final decision as to whether you want to spend the time and money to do a complete analysis for implementing your plan. This assessment is a very high-level review of the data gathering as noted in section 1.1.

For this assessment, we review a basic Initial Questionnaire that takes about 15 to 30 minutes for you to complete online or on hard copy along with an examination of basic documents such as your most recently filed individual and/or corporate tax returns, up-to-date corporate financial statements, RRSPs, and investment statements.

Once we have had the time to review your Initial Questionnaire and financial documents, we can provide you with a very condensed overview of what obstacles and opportunities are available to you based on your desired goals and current situation. In addition, we can give you an estimate of the investment in out-of-pocket costs necessary for you to successfully complete all four phases of your cross-border financial planning.

If you decide that the prepared analysis works for you, you can continue on a cross-border planning process. However, if you find there is not a sufficient cost-benefit value for you and your family, you have not wasted your time, energy, and unnecessary future costs.

If you would like to contact us, or join cross-border discussions forums and groups, visit our website, like us on Facebook, follow us on Twitter, or join us on LinkedIn. You can post basic questions on our forums, which will be answered quickly and without charge. The following includes the contact details to tap into our extensive cross-border financial-planning network:

Website: www.keatsconnelly.com or www.keatsconnelly.ca
Email: info@keatsconnelly.com

Arizona Office
3336 N. 32nd Street, Suite 100
Phoenix, AZ 85018-6241
Phone: 1-800-678-5007 (call toll free from anywhere in Canada or the US)

Florida Office
Renaissance Commons
1880 North Congress Avenue, Suite 302
Boynton Beach, FL 33426
Phone: 561-659-7401 or 1-800-678-5007 (call toll free from anywhere in Canada or the US)